New York Nights

STEPHEN GRAHAM

THE GORGE OF GENERAL MOTORS
"Going along 59th Street one approaches lofty mountains."

New York Nights

By

Stephen Graham

Author of "London Nights," "Midsummer Music," "Under London," etc.

Illustrations by
Kurt Wiese

New York
George H. Doran Company

NEW YORK NIGHTS
— B —
PRINTED IN THE UNITED STATES OF AMERICA

THIS BOOK IS
AFFECTIONATELY DEDICATED
to
PATRICIA

Certain of these chapters have appeared in *Harper's Magazine* and in the *New-Yorker,* to the editors of which acknowledgment is made.

S. G.

Contents

CONTENTS

Illustrations

New York Nights

CHAPTER I

Broadway

BROADWAY is the mother of Broadways all over the world, mother of the lights of Piccadilly Circus and of the Place Pigalle and Teatralny Ploshtchad. The Great White Way is the greatest white way. Those who have never seen it may think that its wide street of automobiles and its thronged pavements were white or that its buildings were marble. But the whiteness is not reality, it is transfiguration; it is the suffusion of floods of soft electric light. A little light is arresting, a little more is staring, more still is annoying, but Broadway has left these stages behind. It has more light by night than it has by day. The blind are aware of some extra luminosity when they are taken along it. One could almost surmise that upon occasion on Broadway at night the blind had received their sight. Miracle is usually attended by light, and, per contra, this marvellous light of Broadway might cause miracle.

Broadway is a great place of health. It is a free electric-ray treatment. It is a tonic light-bath. Almost every one in the world feels better in health when he leaves the cross-streets and the inferior avenues to bask in the great open space in front of that New York temple, the Times Building. Here voices are clearer, eyes brighter, and the whole body more vivid than anywhere else in New York. Though business is responsible for the gift, business gets washed out of the eyes there in the witching hours. Men may still talk business there after the adding-machine has ceased its clatter, but they talk it in a better way. For light is a strainer to the mind and lets thoughts go through clearer. And the pleasure-snared are spiritualised there, and lovers who commonly seek the dark, enjoy and suffer by the infiltration of light.

I sometimes think that the crowds, fused as they are by gaiety, contain numbers of solitary people, friendless and lonely men and women, who have moped all day in wretched gloomy rooms, in homes which are mocked by the happy idea of home. At eleven o'clock at night they bethink them of the radiant shore just so many blocks away, pick themselves out of their loneliness, and make for the light, to lose themselves in the light-intoxicated throngs. Poe's man in the crowd is walking there every night, back and forth, forward and back again, his eyes lit by some dream.

The disillusioned are there to recapture their illusions; the childless, how many with children of their own are still childless, there to find their lost children; the orphans to find that humanity is but one family, and that in truth there is no such thing as an orphan in the world.

The Paramount Building, like some great cocoanut palm, leans indulgently over the Hotel Astor. The theatres debouch their pirouetting pushing half-dazed men and women. Their con-

PARAMOUNT BUILDING
(Near view.) Like superimposed brick-kilns the Paramount blunders upward to the moon.

centrated footlight stare melts to the grandeur of a vaster better-lit stage. They are adjusting and adjusting the lenses of their eyes while they push their way to the freer spaces. The long trains of raging cabs and cars roar and surge like impeded water-courses, but the laughter and light talking of the crowds dissolve their discords, hoots and impatiences. New York is greater than its chauffeurs as Venice than its gondoliers.

No such habitual concourse of multitudes can be seen anywhere else in the world. Londoners do not come together in such numbers except on special occasions such as New Year's Eve at St. Paul's or Armistice Day at the Cenotaph. Parisian boulevards are pale and meagre by comparison. If the lights of Broadway are the great First Cause of the crowds coming into being there is an answering influence from the crowds themselves. The thousands of light-filled eyes repay from their hidden reserves. Humanity is also shedding light, and it wells upward into that other artificial light which is greater than day, a marriage of humanity and life.

But it is not real. The philosopher spurns its actuality and turns back in mind to Manhattan Island as it was and to humanity as it is, was, and shall be, without decoration and shams, the mass of melancholy straddling bipeds so ashamed of themselves that they forever resort to disguises. The philosopher is in part right. It is not real. What is it? It is theatrical. The theatres have disgorged their gazers and listeners, and these have crossed the footlights and have all become actors themselves. That is true. All men and women are actors. Some divine their rôles better than others, but all love the limelight. They love the artifice of night. It gives greater scope than the naturalness of day. They love to mouth it on the stage and gesticulate as they go along. They are prouder of their make-up than of their faces, of what they seem than what they are.

I have only a walking-on part in this great show, and so have time to look about me and criticise. At one thing I especially marvel, that is, at the lighting effects. There is no garishness, no glaring competition of lights. New Yorkers know how to act their parts, but they are greatly helped by the stage and the setting. My commonest reflection as I walk up and down the Great White Way is that somewhere behind the scenes there is a marvellously gifted producer.

CHAPTER II

Night Life

NEW YORK may not be America but it is New York. And New York stands outside comparison. It is without doubt one of the most remarkable places existent now, and one of the most remarkable in history. It is a portent of this and the coming time, the towering apex of a growing pyramid of civilisation. At the same time it is not natural. In some respects it is grander than Nature, for there is more to marvel at in a skyscraper than in a mountain, and there is the illusion of more light flashing off its dynamos than from the revolving sun itself. It is a monument of human artifice. Mankind has built on Manhattan Island something which is almost intolerable, something which has been less hostile to the simplicity of the human soul, but which becomes hourly more insupportable.

For, the higher the houses the smaller the people; the greater the general noise the less the human voice; the more exultant the mechanism the more depressed the organism.

New York spells stress; civilisation spells strain. Nowhere is there greater stress upon millions of people, nor greater strain. Life becomes unlivable, the heart abhors what is called life. It is a city for men, for adolescents only, not for the child in man and woman; a city of prose, of no fairy tales, of ruled lines, of no lore, a city of rigidity, not of wavering and fantastic shapes. New York is a fortress—and how shall the soul escape?

I walked the streets of New York a long while before I found poetry. There was majestic and glittering prose, but no glamour, no softness, no tenderness, no emotional relief even in the secret after-midnight hours, sanctified by the sleeping, by the invincible stars and the quietude of the rivers.

The memory of the day persisted through the night, like pavement heat which robs cities of the relief of sundown. I could understand the remark so commonly made even by those who like New York, that they would never choose it as a city in which to live—in which to be resident and spend their life. To the visitor it can be stimulating beyond any other city. And to the worker returning after his vacation it is another tonic beyond what he has found on the mountain or the sea. It has the stimulus of the Casino where a man will at first be intoxicated by winning and go on to lose much more than he has won. It liberates energy in a human being, and then takes that energy and much more than it has created.

This at least is one true impression of New York, and it caused a writer and observer to think indulgently of the relaxations of the people of the city. Do not attack men's pleasures; attack first the type of work that preceded the pleasure. In our taut modern life we shall not grudge men and women the escapes that they make. A great deal of New York night life is purely escape from New

PAUL WHITEMAN
His baton conducts the lesser lights of Broadway.

York. The side-walks of New York, about which there is the charming sentimental song, are still the runways of business. You take a step to one side, pass a doorway, and you are in a different world. There is a different runway where dancing girls flutter and beckon and sing to a calling crowd. You look at the sea of men's faces, turned towards pleasure as flower-cups to light, and if you are not merely censorious you realise that their drab daily life makes them need illusion at night.

The night club disenchants New York. You pass the portals of a guarded house, leave the throngs in the Avenue, and straightway you are transported to another clime. You are in a village street in Millen, Georgia, with wisps of cotton blowing about. There is dancing in the village square. But it is not Millen of to-day, not of the twentieth century. Old wooden lamp-posts stand round the square, with smoky kerosene lamps in the quaint lanterns above. Lamp-dazzled Emperor moths are on the wing, and float above in the dim light. Men and women sit about at tables, talking or listening or merely existing. It is a Southern night with all the enchantment of indolence, of dusky faces, of soft music, easy laughter and song.

There are tall slender lime trees about the village square. The soft black sky above them is sombre pleated cloth. There are owls with silver plumage and blue diamond eyes looking from the walls. It is only light enough for the eyes to see and rest. A group of Negroes are singing a Dixie song, and the Negroes are like slaves and they are like children. They are fondly unified in a sentimental group, and they croon and beguile with notes of long-drawn sweetness and sadness, telling of another country, a mythical Africa or a never-realised Mother-land, where the corn is so yellow that pure gold is refined, where the birds you cannot hear in Manhattan warble sweetly, where there are flowers so perfect as to produce the melting mood in man, where there is an idleness as of heaven, where our troubles are as nought, where some one, Mother or Mammy, sweetheart or corn-fed bride or "baby" is waiting for us, praying for us.

Outside the night club roll the surface cars, the automobiles hoot, the shop-signs glare, the overhead trains crash on all night, the second shift of workers in the factories gives way to the third shift, the machinery which drives men murmurs intently, persistently, regularly, like a pulse. But inside all is unreality, sentiment, indulgence and relaxation. New York has been banished. Trap-doors have been opened and the tall buildings have gone down under the rock. The sky-signs have faded out. Even the watchful stars are erased, and soft Dixie stars have taken their place. The Go-get-it spirit has gone, and the Let-it-go spirit has taken its place. Time has ceased to be money. Money has ceased to be the great desirable. News sheets have ceased to brazen forth ill-luck. Time and money and news have slipped away, and their urgencies become forgotten. In their place is dreamland, or Nirvana, or a Mussulman's paradise where houris beguile.

Out prance the "Brown Skin Vamps" in a naked children's romp, saffron-coloured silhouettes gliding from lamp-post to lamp-post, posturing, frolicking, showing off. In a primitive community in the Wild West such a show might result in brutal interference on the part of exuberant males. Some "hard guy" would leap the railings. But the slaves of civilisation in New York are not hot-blooded. They are at most warm. Many go to be warmed up, being rather cold. They may have unspent balances at the bank but not unspent physical reserves. Sex appeal is akin to "twilight sleep," it brings about merely twilight awakening. It is languorous and sweet and indulgent and inactive.

After the Vamps have danced the audience still dances. It waltzes indolently to the strains of Irving Berlin's lachrymose love song—

> Though you left a tear
> As a souvenir
> It doesn't matter, dear,
> Because I love you.

The love-mate is not fiercely desired. She has become a "sweetie" or a "baby," some one to fondle and pet. And the terrible male has become merely a beau or also a "baby," or even, horrible expression,—"sugar-daddy." The moon is arranged by Nature for lovers, but this in the Dixie Night Club is a dancing under an artificial moon. Ordinary moonlight is a visionary unreal light, and living in it is living in a reflection. But in the small hours of the night in the dance club it is mock moonlight. A curious contrast Broadway out-blazing the sun, and the night club out-doing the moon with its dim half-light.

This is an impression of the Cotton Club. But if you go to a very different type of resort, say Gipsy Lands on a Thursday night, there is a similar illusion. At the time of writing Thursday night is the great night. Gipsy Lands is Hungarian. I think that for all the hyphenated, for all the foreign elements in the great city New York tiredness expresses itself in a special form of ennui, and that that ennui is a sort of homesickness, a yearning for the old home in Europe, a yearning for an idealised old home. No one really wants to go back, all they want is to dream of going back. It is just as sentimental and unreal as the Dixie dream.

Gipsy Lands,* high up on Second Avenue, has the aspect of a political club. You seem to be over-seriously scrutinised as you enter the dark doorway. No illuminated sign tells you where it is and bids you enter. I suppose the proprietor does not advertise. He does not want the general

* Since writing this Gipsy Lands has been padlocked, gone higher up the Avenue and changed its name.

public so much as his own people. The people who enter help to sustain the character of the place for they are mostly Central European. Without them, the big hall is dreary and its painted walls garish and irrelevant. But with them an illusion of being in Transylvania is produced—Trans-Oceania and Transylvania in one.

Nearly every one inside the club seems to be talking either Hungarian or German. It is part of the ritual to fling off English and revert to the mother-tongue at night, that mother-tongue with all its tender associations. Modern America is checked in with hat and coat at the door, and a freed human being strolls up the narrow ways between the red and white chequered cloth table-tops. There is considerable hubbub of mixed parley, which even the music does not silence. The fine orchestra is playing Hungarian and German music, and the first violin supreme above his fellows and all listeners harmonises the murmur of conversation, making every Hungarian voice among the guests an instrument under his musical sway and leadership.

There are enormous pictures of mountain and gipsy life on all the walls. In fact, the walls are entirely taken up by these brightly coloured landscapes. There is no bit of wall obtruding itself, no vestige of the masonry of the city. The soul finds itself in a new setting. A way of escape has been provided out of the great clamorous bondage of New York into the charm and freedom of a little Hungary—just beyond a black doorway on Second Avenue.

And when Gipsy Lands is full of people the illusion is complete. The life-size figures of gipsies on the walls become alive. They also somehow have come in from the Avenue. They are taking part in the gala night. The leading violinist is performing the miracle. He threads with living music the bending, waving, talking, laughing, crowd and joins scores of conversations. He wins song from them at last, and all break into long-drawn sighing, triumphing chorus. The violinist then slips away like a nurse who has sung a baby to sleep, and in his place the player of the great dulcimer becomes dominant. The dulcimers are sounding, the dulcimers are sounding, the people are singing, yes, even the gipsies who have stepped out of the pictures on the walls are singing the choruses outside their tents. It is two in the morning. It is Hungary. Brazen New York has dissolved in a cocktail. The unreal has become the real—the Hungary of the hungry heart, the imaginary, fantastic, ever-beloved fallacious Hungary, has been created, the sentimental other home. The stress of New York has made Hungarian hearts do this.

One of the most charming places in which to eat in New York is called Samarkand. It is hung with rose-red Persian silks and strange-looking Oriental lamps are suspended from the roof. It is very small—just a casket—and it is served by very charming Russian ladies, probably emigrés of the Russian Revolution. The silk-clad orchestra is perched in a sort of dove-cote above the height of the door.

One night I listened to Chaliapin's great song "Haulers on the Volga," sometimes called "The Volga Boat Song," and was much impressed by the sentimental dreamlike rendering of it. It is really a song of labour, of effort. It is folk-music taken from the lips of the strongest men in the world, the bargee peasants who with ropes about their middles tow various heavy crafts along the Volga stream, walking the soft bank in heavy rhythmic laborious steps and singing to unify their efforts and to feel that all are pulling together.

But at Samarkand those *ai-uchniems* were entirely dissociated from work, and sounded like love-calls of birds in Spring. The song was sung by a real Russian of charming voice. It reminded of Russia. It took the thoughts far away from New York, but to an entirely unreal sentimental Russia, where there was no mud and no labour and no poverty and no rags, no social movements, no rebelliousness. But it satisfied. That was what the diners at Samarkand required—something as far from New York as a wonder city of Central Asia, something as far from labour as a love song.

The Russians have the most enchanting foreign resorts in New York. I doubt if I had more pleasure anywhere than at the Russky Medvied, which is a sort of outpost of East Side gaiety. Not at the dinner crush. There is a very cheap dinner served, and the cabaret is crowded out with lively people going on afterwards to the Houston Street Burlesque and other shows. They bring New York in with them, and there is too much New York to get dissolved in the cup. But when they have gone the Russky Medvied becomes itself. Occasional people, mostly Russian, sit over their tea and lemon and dream, while a divine orchestra of balalaikas and violins takes them back to Russia, to the forests, the birch-trees, the little churches, the ever-touching Russia of poetry, ballad, church-music and folk-tale.

Here also the natural walls are painted out, though not so felicitously as in Gipsy Lands. The birch trees so loved of the Russians, the national trees of Russia, are of course depicted with all tenderness. But the rest is an appeal to the merchant. There is a naked but winged chorus girl in the woods. It is a picnic. There is a disarray of dessert and champagne and red muskmelons lying cut open on the grass. The Russian he-bear, the bull-moose of those parts, holds his wine-glass over the *cendré* hair of his picnic companion, his robust appetite and sensual taste contrasting idly with the somewhat cool chaste manners of those who sit at the tables below the pictures, sipping their tea and lemon, balancing their cigarettes and dreaming with the music.

Not far away, but on the other side of the

rushing coursing Avenue is Little Rumania, made famous in part by the custom and pen of Mr. Konrad Bercovici, but much more by the owner Moskowitz, who is one of the most charming Jews I ever met. The most likely place for a proprietor of a restaurant is near the cash register, but Moskowitz is not there. He is almost always behind his dulcimer which he loves like an only child. Little Rumania is not a night club. Again, it is not quite itself till after the dining crowd has filtered out, leaving the habitués behind. Then it changes into a sort of cabaret, and the playing of Moskowitz and the singing of a Jewish chansonist become the attractive features of the place. It is most alive after the theatre, and becomes thronged with artistic elements of the East Side. It is a marvellous little safety-valve, and its entrance is a trap-door leading away from one of the most commercial regions of the city, for where is there such a massed competition of small shops as on the lower East Side?

Moskowitz told me how as a boy he had begun earning money playing a dulcimer on the ferryboat going between Vraila and Galatz on the Danube. His father used to wait at one of the landing places and take most of the money, leaving him a tiny margin, and from that day to this he has been spiritually wedded to a dulcimer. He is a venerable figure on the East Side now, and his dulcimer seems to have grown with him. The instrument in Little Rumania is much too big and too valuable to be taken by a boy of fourteen to play on a ferry-boat.

But his restaurant remains a sort of ferry. His doorway is a landing-stage, and as you step inside you begin to glide insensibly but steadily away from New York. For nothing that the musicians play expresses the soul of the great city. It expresses escape, it expresses illusion, desire, yearning,

> O that I had the wings of a dove
> Then would I fly far away and be at rest.

And when the soloist sings "Jassa! Jassa!" the fat ladies at the tables slap their bare arms with their palms and sing it in chorus too. Even Jassa is more desirable than Manhattan. At night all the Jews go back, and this time Moskowitz is their Moses.

Don Dickerman is another of the pleasure-vendors of New York who has cleverly commercialised the desire for illusion. Every one enjoys the Country Fair, its gaiety, its colour, its fustian and its freaks, its robust if vulgar music. Dickerman told me he once played the part of the "Man-Mangling Human Gorilla" at Maine County Fair, and it gave him an idea for his resort on East Ninth Street. There the guests all get into quaint booths ticketed "Zisco that Strange Girl," "Maniac Marmaduke and Family," "Kiss Me" and the like, and the place is all alive with hanging bunting, freak-shows, cockshies and so forth, and a good band very rurally clad.

Dickerman has also produced the Pirates' Den. He was with William Beebe on one of the Arcturus expeditions and brought back to New York some remarkable marine curiosities. These figure in the Pirates' Den. It is rather a boyish night club. All the waiters are disguised as pirates of the 18th century, and except for their mild eyes and blameless mouths are a fearsome looking crowd. They stage scenes from "Treasure Island," and ship brawls, they fire shots, break into outrageous talk, start old-fashioned disputes and clash cutlasses. The den is dark. It has its wonderful parrot. You drink cider from old mugs and stare at full-bodied sailors in cotton vests and corded breeches and knee boots with hanging leather flaps, at the walls of the smoky cellar hung with maps, toy-ships, fishes' skeletons, whales' vertebræ, picks from Cocos Island and pirates' signatures cut on rocks. Suddenly there is a squall of thunder and lightning, and the band and its platform raised by pulleys begin to mount to the upper deck. The sound of a ship's bell breaks through the noise of the mock storm. Voices are heard from various parts of the imaginary ship. "All quiet on the main deck, sir!" . . . "Forward light burning bright!" . . . "Prisoners safe in the brig!"

"Good kid stuff, don't you think?" enquires

Dickerman, admiring his own artifice. "All this appeals to the everlasting boy in the grown man. It gets him, he likes to forget business and that he is grown up, and be a boy again."

I think of the words of the poet "Come, be a child once more" as invisibly written over the portals of the Pirates' Den. Not that New York people need the invitation. They are very ready to be children again. I was at a dinner of the New York Bar once and listened to eminent judges singing "A long long trail of winding" in chorus. I have even been to a church where they sang "Jingle Bells" instead of a hymn. It is all part of the great escape from the too serious life which the grown-up world has invented.

In the New York dawn the cabs are drawn up outside the Night Clubs. Miss Guinan still stands on her chair in her enchanted grotto on 54th Street and indulgently pets the lost children of the city who have come to her. Or Barney Galant drinks his liquorice and water and loquaciously banters the relaxed and sweetened revellers of Greenwich Village. Nigger Heaven, away up in the hundred-and-thirties, begins to dim its stars. The sun heaves upward revengefully crimson and self-conscious, urgently hastening the banishment of Night. The toilers stream along the cross-town streets. The long arms of cranes become visible swinging great stones into position in the new tall buildings. "We are only beginning," say the machines. The New York of to-morrow is imperiously calling. New Yorkers—you shall go higher, you shall go faster. "Yes," says the New Yorker in his heart, "but at nights we shall deny the visions of the day."

New York is not America, but it is New York. New York night life is not even New York. It is a hidden chamber in the kingdom of the heart. Draw the blinds! Light the lamps!

CHAPTER III

Exterior Street

I STARTED off from South Ferry one night upon a zigzag walk. Sleepless tramps were huddled in the seats in Battery Park; others were lying on the grass, flat and dazed as if they had fallen from balloons. There were hoots and howls from across the river, red lights and green lights, the hum-grum of machinery, and the strange electric-light cascade of moving elevated trains. 'Twas one by the clock. Syria slept. Greece slept.

I walked by Front Street to Moore Street, to Water Street, to Broad, to Pearl, to Coenties Slip, to Stone, to Mill Lane, to South William Street, to Broad again, past a blank empty lighted telegraph office, to Exchange Place, to New Street, to Wall Street. Thus I arrived at the financial anvil of the world. But all was still, no hammering, no bellows blowing, no flying sparks. Yellow stars looked down on the deserted Exchange. But I saw what appeared to be some Pagan temple, a stark altar of human sacrifice, and it proved to be a famous Christian Church, none other than Holy Trinity on Broadway, and as I stood by the strange little graveyard the church clock struck half past one. The little white headstones looked like the dead popping up from the tomb. There was heard the resounding hoot of a steamer on the river—yea, the last trump. Fast cars scooted along wet empty Broadway as if fleeing the wrath to come—and all were going up town.

Then I went on by Little Thames Street, and felt for a moment as if I were in part of the City of London. It also is deserted in the regions of Capel Court at that hour of the night. There are no night-shifts in stockbroking. You do not see a relief of stenographers being marched up Wall Street by a Managing Clerk; the stenographer's relief is prancing in the White Friars and Tango-land.

I was in Cedar Street and Greenwich Street, walking under the "El" like a rat, and came to Liberty Street—O Liberty, most empty was thy street—and to Washington above that sleeping Syria and sleeping Greece, and so, going by Cortland Street, I came to West Street and its great market. It was two o'clock, and New York here was very much alive.

There were horse waggons and motor waggons, cases and baskets of vegetables and fruit, and porters innumerable hurrying hither and thither with gleaming white-wood boxes on their shoulders. I emerged from the dead city where never a blade of grass twinkles before square toes and came into a fairyland of cucumbers and corn, cabbages and melons and Malaga grapes. Refreshing fruit odours invaded the nostrils.

Heaps of small black grapes looked in the dim light like exaggerated caviare. I kicked a peach as I walked along. What largesse in the night, peaches are like stones in the roadway! They tumbled from wooden troughs and buckets uncovered and overfilled. There were South Mountain oranges and California lemons. There were crates of greens stacked higher than men. There were cabinets of blackberries and raspberries. The nose whispered to the heart "Raspberries, raspberries" as it tasted the air. Coloured porters with perspiring gleaming faces shouldered boxes of green varnish-surfaced peppers along narrow alley ways between piles of other boxes. Carrots peeped out of their ventilated crates like brown ribbons. Side streets were blocked with potatoes and yams. Activity, activity, activity—and quietude. The workers do not help themselves along with foul expletives and abuse as in London. They seem to be conserving their energy, or imitating the electric lamps which do their job and say nothing about it. But it is a big market, bigger than Covent Garden in London, and I reflected that New Yorkers eat more fruit and vegetables than we do. There is more for them to eat. Their reserves are greater.

The quayside beyond the market is long and spacious and empty. The freer air seems to be minus something—is it the mental ozone of New York? West Street is a long backyard. It has no mechanical turnings on the left. If you wish to take a turning on the left, the way of the heart, you must take a ship. There are ships in the wharves still as birds dozing head on wing in a covert at

FROM THE HUDSON AT NIGHT

Palaces and temples of commerce, prophetic and murmuring by day, awe-striking by night.

night. Not a rustle nor a whisper comes from the giant Cunarder. West Street is the landing stage of the Atlantic ferry. You stand on West Street and you think Southampton. You stand in West Street and you think Havana, San Juan, Cristobal, Panama, Valparaiso. You stand on West Street and think Cherbourg, Naples, the Piræus. But now no one is thinking anything. The gangways may be down, but no one is on them. Eastward New York's luminosity lies in layers like masonry of light and darkness built from the rocks to the night-sky. Westward lies the beautiful river flowing away to the calm ocean. And on the wide roadway of the quay laden lorries rush and crash bearing produce to the market or away.

I sought a turning on the left and did not find one till Fourteenth Street. It was a lonely walk. A drunken man sitting on a bit of paving addressed me vaguely. He was looking at the heavens with lack-lustre eye.

"There's only one star left. How far's that from here?" he queried.

I passed an empty "Goulash Kitchen," passed standing freight cars, passed the embarkation for Tampa and Mobile, passed the Boston and Providence pier, passed the R. M. S. P., passed the Hoboken Ferry and entered the Gansevoort market stirring feebly. A black and white cat was squatting in the roadway fastidiously eating melon.

My turning to the left proved to be the virtual one of Eleventh Avenue where it starts North near

West Fourteenth Street, and there, like a derelict trolley car left stranded on the ooze after the subsidence of a flood, was a windowed shed with the explicit word LUNCH printed on it. This was kept by a lonely Greek.

"Where do you come from?" I asked, perched on my revolving stool at the counter and munching pie.

"Island," he answered.

"What? From Ireland? You don't look it."

"No. Island. Crete. Greek, yes."

"Fine country."

"No. Some nations go up. Some nations go down. The great Alexander thousand year ago take whole world. Then Venetians come. Before Jesus. Romans. Yes, the French. Napoleon. Germans. Now English, I guess."

"Not Americans?"

"No, English now. But in two hundred year maybe England go down. Other nation rise up."

"How d'ye like New York?"

"Not like it. Bad place here. Kill you for a dime. Want woman; cost ten dollars. Take her hotel two more. Drinks bad poison. Good drink cost big money. Not like New York."

A friend from the island of Rhodes rolled in for his morning coffee on his way to work at the National Biscuit Factory. "Rhodes no good. Italians there. They turn out Greeks. New York fine. Plenty money. Rodos bad."

I said Good Morning and Good-bye, and

walked out on to Fourteenth Street, turned into Tenth Avenue and then into West Fifteenth Street where the "fleet" of the Biscuit Company was waiting in the dark like a string of camels before dawn on the outskirts of Baghdad.

Biscuits are not made all night. They are evidently partly compounded of daylight. But here was where my friend from Rhodes belonged, or in local parlance here the islander "held down his jahb."

Ninth Avenue was drear. Orion up above the roofs was striding hastily across Sixteenth Street. On Eighth Avenue a big fruiterer's stood wide open, very still and empty. What zest for trade!

West Seventeenth Street, Seventh Avenue, West Eighteenth, Sixth Avenue, West Nineteenth, passed as one. I was thinking of London and did not notice them. At Fifth Avenue I paused, for the speedway had had its nightly wash and was all aswill with water like a bath-house floor.

I zigzagged across to Lexington and saw an iceman dragging blocks of ice into a large clean-swept and ready but empty cafeteria. On Twenty-third Street I stopped at a shop window which was stacked with dollar shirts. A tall notice said "FORCED TO SELL." The shop was closed but it was flooded with electric light. I saw many offices and barber shops where the lights had been left on all night. And on Twenty-ninth Street I paused in front of a locked undertaker's where a white-lined baby's coffin was exposed, charmingly illuminated.

On Avenue A, the ashpan of the other avenues, there were notices which struck an Englishman as strange. The words TRANSIENTS met my eye. We advertise "Short Garage" but New Yorkers talk of "Transients." What poetry there is in the word! In some streets all other lighted signs have been put out and the one word remains brilliantly enshrined, now here, now there, "Transients!" "Transients!"

After all, every one in the great caravanserai of New York is a transient. Every one in the caravanserai of the world is a transient. The world itself is a transient. Look up among the stars; you will see it as a celestial sky sign. There it is pricked out all over the dark deep of space—TRANSIENTS.

I am a transient in the city of New York at night. I am gyrating across the fitfully sleeping city from the Hudson to the East River. No other great city can be got across so quickly. One could run across it in less than half an hour. I was soon out at the water edge on the other side of the island, listening to the ceaseless Edison works. Oh, what is Edison contriving there, are they engines of death or of life? The wonder name of Edison stirs the imagination as if he were an arch wizard, the Michael Scott of the New World. The river of Time flows by and the great works climb upward on its banks.

It is five a.m. Something of the burden of the city has been lifted. The air is light. The heart seems freed. I feel happy to be walking. I love the space and the quietness. I have got rid of the idea of going to bed, got rid of the routine of daily life. New York and its millions, its wealth, its mysteries, are mine. There is a sense of conquest. The bustle has died down and I am still walking. The majority of people are asleep—but I am not the least sleepy. It seems as if life has just begun. I am dancing on a springed floor. The stones of the side-walks help me to leap along First Avenue, grim, empty, gloomy Avenue One, which has no turning to the right except little bottle-neck lanes which go down to the edge of the water of the East River.

I spent many nights in this way wandering about the city and returning at dawn, resuming next night at the point where I had left off the night before.

Whoever would know the poetry of New York must walk it in the after-midnight hours, see the red light come out on the Metropolitan tower preliminary to the striking of the hour; one is too pre-occupied and diverted to observe it in the livelier hours; enter the Central station at four a.m. and see it anew, deserted, silent, beautiful as on the morning of Opening Day; see the City Hall at dawn hanging down from on high like the sky's apron.

Queensboro Bridge, seen from the foot of East Fifty-third Street late at night, is a marvellous spectacle. There is light in the sky above and wandering light on the river below. There is all the grandeur which circumambient shade can give. "What have I come to?" you ask, astonished after the sordidness of the Avenue, with its many garbage cans. Suddenly you see a mirage. It is called Queensboro Bridge. It takes the mind to the finest parts of the Seine and the Thames. You feel you must be at the centre of a great city, near its Parliament, its palaces, its pontifical grandeurs. But this is Rome without a Pope—a mere bridge, beautiful and awe-inspiring by accident, a convenience whose formal magnificence goes unheeded in the daytime, when business absorbs all the interest and takes the first and only place in men's eyes.

Still as I walk on I find the influence of the bridge expressed in men's habitations. As I approach the great viaduct of the bridge the poor district smartens up dramatically. The massive piles of the viaduct and the lofty exaggerated attendant factory chimneys, the vague Colossus of a gas works, all suggest more spacious living, and Sutton Place is the reply.

But I descend rapidly a long straight empty street nameless here for evermore, and it becomes Avenue A—the old ashpan once again. People of no social prominence are herded in grim unremarkable blocks. Fire ladders disfigure the houses, or do they merely hide them, like black veils the ravaged faces of elderly ladies. Perhaps the houses look worse than a similar variety in

London. But imagine Bow and Whitechapel all festooned with rusty fire ladders! There is something queer about these ladders. They look like the old black ladders of tramp steamers let down to the wharves. The immigrant never gets away from the debarkation gangway. All New York is a quay. I see all the vessels that have arrived there—then the population swarming on the streets are all people who have come off ships.

But it is the most extraordinary shore in the world. It is well to have arrived there sometime or other on life's voyage.

Solitary walking along the empty streets seems to attune the mind to the city. True thoughts flow like music from the mind. I came to another outside street happily named Exterior Street. It has a Venetian view of river, lights, ferries, and small boats. Away beyond the river the sparse lights of Welfare Island diamond the dark. On the right is the grandeur of the bridge. But Exterior Street is below New York. It is bounded by the great grey cliff of the original Manhattan Island. Somewhere up above there are houses and gardens. Children perhaps come and drop pebbles down into Exterior Street or on to the shaggy tufts of old grass. It is like a bit of mountain road. There are hunks of uncontrolled rock. The shoulder of the world juts out. The silence is only accented by the rustling of the wind. No, there is another sound which is part of the silence, it is the undying whirr of rotary machines. I am walking towards a huge factory and from its little doors strange dwarfs with darkened faces come out, look round, and go in again—the workers, they don't belong. I sit on the grass under the cliff and look over the water. It is Exterior Street: I am outside New York.

To understand any experience you must get outside of it.

King Canute went to Exterior Street and bade the waves keep away from his toes. The gentry from Park Avenue and Upper Fifth might well make a pilgrimage to Exterior Street at four in the morning and sit there in the grass, outside the scene of their wealth and their power.

I left this curious street by smart residential East Seventy-ninth, thence by East End Avenue to East Eightieth. I had been *outside;* soon I was very much *inside*. I came to a steaming curtained window, lighted and murmurous. The one word STUBE was explanatory. I went inside and asked for cider. This seemed to amuse the bar-tender who, however, poured out two mugs of it at once and set them before me. There was a big notice on one of the walls, NO GAMBLING, and under it a vociferous throng were throwing scarlet dice.

"Splitz!" "Splitz!"—every one at the bar was asking for "Splitz."

I was invited to join the "Wilhelm Union." No one spoke a word of English. Mine host kept saying something about *zwei kasen Scotch verkauft.* I had a glass of whisky with a red-faced and puffing, very drunken man who showed me an iron cross and very paradoxically wanted to kiss me. I pointed to the only girl in the establishment, sitting sulkily in a corner. He took me over to a poster depicting the American Unknown Soldier which was inscribed—"Work for the Living," and he nodded his head sententiously. A fig for unknown soldiers; all German soldiers were unknown. At least, so I surmised.

In this tavern ended another night and when next I resumed I quickly reached luxuriant, spacious, Southern-looking Fifth Avenue, *the* Avenue, as it is affectionately called. Curious fact about the avenues—the word avenue means approach; in England avenues are usually bordered with trees; in order to make a road into an avenue you plant trees. An avenue's trees are its guard of honour leading to the portals of country house, castle, or palace. But the avenues of New York do not lead anywhere. They are paved rivers which go on and on through various districts to lose themselves eventually in wildernesses, to be dried up in social deserts. But Fifth Avenue for one hundred and ten streets does preserve its character of grandeur, and it is one of the most exhilarating ways to walk in any city.

With Central Park on one side and fine houses on the other, I walked twenty blocks, the Harlem moon standing over the street and raising gleaming reflections all the way. Moonlight also glinted from the highly polished varnish of fast moving automobiles. No one was walking except myself, and many men and women passed in cars and taxis, mostly lovers indulgently petting one another in course of transit from one night-club to another, or from a dance to their homes.

I turned with the park railings along Hundred-and-Tenth Street and came to the gay base of Lenox Avenue, then went in a circle through the Morningside district back to Fifth Avenue. I came to Harlem all aflare with the lure of pleasure—cabarets, night-clubs, dance-halls, chop-suey restaurants, parlours. At three in the morning I watched a bevy of coloured girls operating a barber shop, cutting the fuzzy hair of Harlem dandies in a brilliantly lighted hairdressing saloon. I strayed into Capitol Club and saw white women dreamily trotting with Negroes in slow jazz, strange women who defy the custom of night to enjoy the sensual thrill of the black man's dance.

By the cross-streets I passed through Africa. Street after street was entirely black, housing swarms of families, all black. Banjoes still throbbed in some; the ukuleles gurgled dance music, but most houses were silent. They were sleeping and snoring. They were bathed in the deep physical ardour of Negro sleep—only in doorways here and there petting couples lingered awake, oblivious of the clock.

I left Harlem by Edgecombe Avenue and St. Nicholas Avenue, the road dug up and dotted with red lanterns, and came to a substantial quiet and English-looking neighbourhood, Hamilton Terrace, 144th Street and Convent Avenue, very respectable.

But respectability only held a strip, and having crossed it I was in Amsterdam Avenue. Then I came to Broadway still very much Broadway and, making a sharp descent by 147th Street, came once more to the end of New York—the grandest backway of all—Riverside Drive. The view was very beautiful. I could imagine that the Hudson River was the Danube and that I was in Bratislava again. The esplanade was high, serene, and wind-blown, fresh with raindrops flickering across the eyes. Little boats, like sleeping ducks, lay upon the surface of the water. The automobiles which whirled along the drive seemed unreal; the river is the great reality. It is on view here. It knows it was before all the rest and will survive it, with thousands of years both before and after.

A ferry boat crosses the river like a tram on the sea—transients once more, transients. Three shooting stars follow and pass over New Jersey—transients, transients. All is transient. New York is a setting for a drama that is being played, a spectacle which is being rehearsed. At four in the morning I am walking along like the Wandering Jew, but my taste is shared by two lovers in a solemn closed car drawn up overlooking the river. Through the misty glass I see them in one another's arms, in close embrace.

Through silver-tinted clouds the moon seems

to beat her way, keeping coming out, keeping going in, and as I climb Washington Heights I seem to be making another exit from the city, upward to the stars. All the way from South Ferry to the sky—I have skated the stairways of the city. I have gone from outside to inside, by Exterior Street to the heart. The mystic closes his eyes that he may see better. The curtain which comes down gives leisure to the mind to consider the hidden springs of drama. Night reveals the day.

CHAPTER IV

My Partners

A PRETTY partner is the best passport to New York at night. With the right sort of lady on your arm you can obtain admittance into any resort, even the most guarded and exclusive. With her you do not need to "crash," to use an expression commonly heard near night-club doors. It is a sad comment on chivalry, but plain-looking women are looked upon with suspicion. *Place aux dames* has given way to *Place aux jolies femmes.* In America most plain women have the cause of Woman or of public morals at heart. They are ardent temperance reformers and belong to purity leagues. So door-men have orders to exclude them. I tested this with a severe intellectual friend who used to be the partner of a man on a radical weekly paper and found that doormen were shy of her.

At first in New York I went about by myself and that had several advantages. I was able to walk the city up and down. No one wants to walk far in New York; taxis are numerous and cheap. The New Yorker has no feet. But the taxi closes off the view. You feel some bumps and you surmise you are on 8th Avenue, or a blaze of light tells you that you are on Broadway. And as for subways and Elevated trains, they seem to destroy both time and scene. I also found it advantageous to go to certain speakeasies alone. At the cost of one bad drink I saw all there was to be seen, whereas with a companion it might have been necessary to drink several. But New York is not a lonely man's city; it is social or it is nothing. The lively places are the more interesting. For these one must have a suitable partner. You do not have half as much of an adventure by yourself as you do with a friend.

There were Patricia and Helen. I owe so much to Pat that I have dedicated this book to her and I owe a great deal to Helen, too. Amusing and striking the difference between being at Texas Guinan's with a partner and being there without one. Without one you are a *gigolo*.

Patricia sold film-rights of novels and helped edit a magazine. Helen was an artist on the "World." One wrote a monthly article of gossip; the other was responsible for a Sunday "strip." Many of our adventures found reflection in the articles and the strip. It is charming to take out girls who are earning their living. Their day experiences enriched night conversations. Had they been ordinary revellers they would never have got up till lunch the next day, but Pat even after all night festivity seemed fresh and fit at her office in the morning.

I danced first with Helen at the Villa Venice, one of the more refined of the fashionable resorts in the neighbourhood of the Plaza Hotel. Probably it is not fashionable at all nor Bohemian, but just middle-class. I think so because drink was not much in view. With Pat I danced first at the

Bamboo Inn, which is an enormous non-descript Harlem cabaret. I was with both Helen and Patricia at the Nest, at Gipsy Lands and at Little Rumania. I danced with Helen at Connie's Inn, at Small's, at Roseland, at the Mirador, at the Pennsylvania Grill and several other places.

Helen and I had walking-on parts at "Broadway" on one occasion and sat at a night-club table on the stage and clinked glasses. Another night we went behind the scenes of the "Circus Girls" at the Winter Garden. We talked to the horses, the chorus girls and the clowns. There was a white horse called Thunder who kept turning off electric lights with his nose. A clown would address him in this wise: "Why can't you leave the light alone? Who do you think you are? You great bum, thinking of nothing but eats. If you don't behave, you'll be a dead horse. We won't put your rhinestone harness on."

And another clown standing by would comment, "Keep away from him. He was a good horse till he met you." The horse turns off another light. "All right. No sugar to-night. The son of a bitch. Shame on you, bad boy, naughty boy. Don't do it. Lissen there. Back up."

And Thunder would raise his upper lip in a quivering grimace asking for sugar.

It was interesting to watch the disarray of chorus girls and clowns and rapid-moving scene-shifters and white madams strutting about in ballet dancers' frills feeding the horses with sugar or brushing archly against grandiosely dressed Grand Dukes or scarlet-coated masters of the hunt. We sat in Hassell's dressing-room while he posed for a drawing, sitting and holding an eyebrow pencil to the brow of his daughter Virginia. It was Virginia's first appearance in New York and her father said he thought her face was too luridly made-up, "like a butcher's shop."

Helen told me that last time she was at the Winter Garden there was an elderly gentleman in a brown derby who sidled up to all the girls in turn, caressing most of them and kissing some. She enquired who he was and was told, "He is the angel of the piece." But this time there was no angel; the Circus Girls were performing without heavenly guidance.

With Patricia I visited many speakeasies. Helen helped me a great deal because she is so very observant and filled out my own impressions by telling me things which I should never have seen. Patricia helped me in a different way. She is the soul of gaiety and enters with such verve into the spirit of night-life that I am not surprised that her nick-name for herself is "the darling of the speakeasies." Sparkling, laughing, intoxicating Pat, I shall never forget you as you were on Armistice Night at Texas Guinan's, strutting about with a white bear-skin which you had borrowed from one of those nearly naked girls, who had been marching to every military air the band could think of. They said, "Texas does not know her job to let you be part of the company and not one of us."

With Patricia I danced at the Lorraine, at Barney's, at Paul Whiteman's and among the palms under the sliding roof of the Club Madrid. We saw the burning of the Netherland Tower together. We went to midnight Mass at the Russian Church on Russian Easter Eve. We had been dining with Robert Milton at his apartment on West 57th Street. He was encouraging us to write a play. Milton, who is a clever producer, is a Russian born near St. Petersburg. I believe he was designed for the priesthood but ran away. He told us amusing stories of his early days when he was on the road with Douglas Fairbanks and others, and they relied on Doug to dazzle farm-wives with his stunts, and thus obtain a "hand-out." He is a whimsical, diverting, ingenious person. We talked and laughed for hours, but it was Russian Easter Eve. So the three of us took a cab and went to Church together.

The Russians in New York are split into at least two factions. The Reds hold the cathedral on 95th Street, taking their lead from atheistic Moscow. It is part of the organization paradoxically named the "Living Church." The Whites have rented a church in which to carry on the true traditions of Orthodoxy. It is the Church of St. Salvador at 121st and Madison. To St. Salvador we went.

At midnight Patricia and I might have been

seen standing wedged in a mass of Russians, listening to many cries of *Christos Voscrece.* We held candles in our hands. I felt very sad. There was little to remind me of Russia. Few people crossed themselves. There were no men in the choir. Women were there uncovered. There were no Easter breakfasts waiting for blessing. My mind went back to Moscow and the night of the eve of my marriage, listening to all the Easter bells, and above all to the booming forth of Ivan Veliky. Mr. Milton's face also was pale and tense as if he were thinking of Russia. Curious to think that we were on the verge of Harlem with all its jazzy activities. In London at the Russian Church on Easter Eve one is entirely in Russia. I suppose the Russian spirit does not thrive in America.

About one in the morning we lost Mr. Milton. Yes, just about the time one turns to one's neighbour to give the Easter kiss he was not to be found. Patricia learned the right answer to "Christ is risen . . ." Yes, He is risen indeed. But instead of giving me the correct salute she looked around for Mr. Milton.

With Pat I went to see the "King of Kings," also to "Deep River," and the "Grand Street Follies," and to the Lafayette Theatre to see Negro burlesque, and to that quaint comedy called "White Wings." Pat learned to sing "White wings they will never grow weary," which was the most popular street song in London when I was a small boy and was revived in this piece.

Many of our nights out were associated with songs. She loved dining at the Russian Bear for the music. We sampled many charming dining places such as Katinka's, the Marine Room, the Hoffbrau House in Hoboken, Manney's Place amid the garbage of Forsythe Street, and Hungaria and Abbazzia in Yorkville. Many resorts were nameless. They were just street-numbers and the best of them was a French restaurant-speakeasy on 51st Street, run it was said in connection with a French ship, a picture of which hung over the zinc bar.

We saw the dawn come up one morning, walking arm in arm on top of a high building, among tiled tepees and strange looking tanks. The roses she had worn all night were still living on a shoulder of her rose-coloured dress, and rose-coloured reflections from the glamorous East softened the staring starch and dead blackness of evening attire seen in the morning. Happiness on many nights lasted over till next day when we might be seen lunching at the Algonquin, and till evening when we would be at Jack's bar, or dining at Hemil's, after that, sitting laughing in a theatre, going from thence to a cabaret, then to another place of dance. I think that in all this we never had a dull moment. Pat was to me the living spark of New York.

CHAPTER V

Speakeasies

THE itinerant bootlegger running around in his car delivers gin at the door at the price of two dollars a bottle. I have one in front of me; it is labelled "HIGH & DRY GIN—BOOTH'S, estd. 1740. *The Original Dry Gin.*" It is marked "Imported for Medicinal Purposes only." In England a similar bottle of Booth's Gin would cost twelve shillings. Gin is very easily made and I have no reason to say either through surmise or experiment that the contents of the bottle are impure. When I needed liquor for a party at my apartment I telephoned Helen's bootlegger, Bobby, and I said plainly just what I wanted and he would run up with it in his car, bacardi at three dollars a bottle, apricot brandy at three-fifty the libre. Most liquor sold by a reputable bootlegger is cheaper in New York than in London. Occasionally a fancy price is asked for some special bottle. There are always people who having paid a high price will find that the liquor is superior and for that reason high prices are exacted. But it is safe to say that in general Prohibition has caused a cheapening of drink in the United States. But in some speakeasies prices are much heavier. I suppose one pays to cover the risk in the barkeeper's business. The customer pays his part of the graft. Nevertheless the profits must be high. You can buy from a bootlegger Sauterne at fifty cents the bottle and you can pay for a similar bottle

AT THE SPEAKEASY RESTAURANT
"What is your name? Was you here before?"

at a restaurant as much as six dollars. I know the wine well enough not to be deceived. I believe real French White wine is very rare in New York; it does not pay to import it. Authentic rum is brought in great quantities from the Indies and that also is very cheap except when bought in a cocktail at a speakeasy.

New York swarms with speakeasies. Some of them are curiously charming places and should survive the Volstead Act if that piece of legislation is ever abrogated. There are many Italian ones half of which are known as "Tony's." Let me describe one to which I went to meet Laura, a poet.

Spy-holes, moving shutters, padlocks, chains, bars, a password . . . the Italians understand well the ritual of the secret society, but the Anglo-Saxon is always rather mirthful over elaborate precaution. One might have thought that Tony belonged to the Black Hand.

But inside his establishment there was nothing frightening. His rooms might have been those of a college girl years ago. Rose-coloured walls, a bust of Dante on the mantelpiece, views of Florence and Rome and of the Leaning Tower of Pisa, thin-legged uncomfortable straight-backed chairs and work-tables. And there was Laura, whom I had promised to meet, sitting at one of the little work-tables contemplating a half-filled glass of crême de rose.

I said that I would ne'er come back,
But here I am, here I am,

she crooned. With her was a young novelist of fame. They had been to the theatre together. A scene in a speakeasy and a dialogue of two theatre-goers discussing the play would make a piquant epilogue for a Broadway play.

The clientele at this bar was mostly of women. Women brought their women friends. Women brought their men friends. Tony accepted men's money but he had I believe a preference for that of the women. It is sometimes an act of gallantry nowadays to take women's money, and in this respect he was gallant. This was a lady's speakeasy.

We sat down to a conversation on the theme: Where is modern woman going? I said, back to the harem and the veil. I contended there would come a time when passive man would arouse himself, declaring that women in their freedom had gone too far, and that a war would be waged for the re-enslavement of the sex. But in my argument I was not supported, and in my pre-vision they did not see with me. Somnolent ladies in charming gowns nodded their heads bibulously at neighbouring tables. Fat cherry-cheeked Tony smiled between rings at the bell. At each ring he went momentarily pale so that those who observed him thought of the police.

He brought me some Benedictine, and the bottle was right. But the liqueur was curious—transparent at the top of the glass, yellowish in the middle, and brown at the base. It was sweet and strong, and I am sure you could not find its like in France.

Oh, what dreams seemed to result from drinking it! Next morning I had no appetite for breakfast. That is the bane of speakeasy life. You ring up your friend next morning to find out whether he is still alive.

When you receive good liqueur you can be sure it is imported. But it seems to me now you need to be a European to be able to decide what is good and what is spurious. Americans are falling into horrid doubt. The best liqueur offered me in New York was in a place off Fifth Avenue kept by three Irish boys. This purported to be 1830 Grand Marnier. "Jack" said it had been consigned to him by mistake, a very small bottle and very expensive. But as the rule of his establishment was a dollar a drink, no matter what you had, he would keep to that price. This was certainly good Grand Marnier, and just as certainly it was imported, not made. There was no doubt of that, though I should not care to say I believed it was nearly a hundred years old; it was dark and rich and powerful. It was very enkindling. This speakeasy was an elegant suite of rooms furnished with broad and soft divans, luxurious armchairs and dim shaded lights, for drinking and precious petting. Jack, the eldest of the three Irish proprietors, gave the opinion that the marriage rate in New York was improving because petting was becoming so expensive. You could not go to a Child's Restaurant to pet, or to one of those places called "Coffee Pots," or to thunderous Thompsons, where there are only bachelor seats, or to a self-serve cafeteria. Lovers cannot hold one another in Bryant Park where the tramps converse, nor at fashionable hotels glared at by tip-hunting waiters. You must do it in a taxi where the meter counts the kisses in dollars and cents, or resort to a night-club or speakeasy where love is assessed in the price of bootleg liqueur. Jack considered that all to the good. He held that petting caused a procrastination of marriage but hindrance of petting hastened it. Still, there are so many dim rooms in New York, with or without cover-charge but certainly with "petting privileges" that I was inclined to doubt Jack's edict that petting was decreasing, though I had an open mind as regards the relationship to the marriage question. Nevertheless I suppose those long intimate after-theatre conversations in the dark corners of Jack's bar were more of love than of marriage.

But the liquor even here where the commendable Grand Marnier was sold was not dependable. The liqueurs were excellent but danger was hidden in the cocktails. One can never be quite sure what will happen to you after a New York cocktail. One night Pat fell a victim to the ingredients of an "old-fashioned cocktail." We dined at a

Rumanian restaurant on the East Side, on "Garnitura" and a bottle of sacramental wine. Then we went to see "Deep River"—the Negro jazz opera, at whose pedantic libretto, a sort of slow-motion Shakespeare, we laughed exceedingly. Thence we went to Jack's who diverted us for hours telling his reminiscences and gossiping about his customers. His chief bootlegger (wholesaler) was a teetotaller who had a discreetly furnished apartment on Park Avenue, with teak cabinets and walls hung with priests' vestments. He was wholly matter-of-fact, conventional, timorous. There was nothing of the sheik or bootleg king. No gunman he! He was not concerned with territorial rights and invisible frontiers like Steve Crandale and Scar Edwards in that gripping melodrama "Broadway." His preoccupation was merely getting the stuff in and getting it distributed, and he was one of the busiest of men—at the telephone.

Another friend of Jack's—a customer—was known as Count Romanof. Some one said to him, "Why, your name is the same as the Tsar's!" He replied, "Oh, yes, my uncle." He was a supposed dealer in Art treasures and he always came with some potential purchaser who stood him the drinks. The likelihood of his being a Romanof was impaired by the story that he used to be known as Prince Serge Obolenski, the one who married the rich Miss Astor, until the real Prince Serge confronted him one day in Paris and gave him confounding evidence of a personal alibi.

Then Jack imitated the talk of "Billy the Kid" and drew a picture of his wife on an old envelope. Billy the Kid was evidently a night bird and a habitué. There are mannerisms of talking which are especially to be associated with the alcohol habit. The lips are more compressed than those of teetotallers who more or less speak with frank open mouths. But Billy the Kid as imitated by Jack did not seem to open his mouth at all.

Jack took personal charge of our drinks. He showed us his bottles assuring us that he was very particular about labels. If he ever received a bottle with a "phoney label" he set it aside and returned it to the wholesaler. But it must be thought that there was some destructive ingredient in his "old-fashioned cocktail" that night unless perchance it was the Rumanian sacramental wine which caused the trouble. The Houston Street vineyards may be suspect. About two-thirty in the morning we took a cab to a Russian cellar. It was supposed to be closed, but upon talking in Russian to one of the out-coming customers we found admittance. Here a Russian was playing a concertina and a man in evening dress was dancing with a highball balanced on his head. His beautifully-gowned partner did not seem to mind the risk she took of being splashed with whisky. If her partner ruined her dress no doubt he would have to buy her three. There were beautiful white swans on the roseate walls. Portly waiters brought forth chicken and rice and skewered bits of mutton smoking hot from the hands of an able Russian chef. Dreamy American couples petted in the corners; garrulous Russians gossiped over drinks, and the young fellow in peasant blouse mixed jazz with folk music as he fingered the concertina. On the shadowy floor the burlesque gentleman hopped to and fro with the glass of whisky on his head.

But my companion had not much interest in this matter or in the interesting couples in this rose-lighted Caucasian den; she was ill. Her face was white; she trembled. We ordered black coffee but it remained untasted. There was nothing for it but to put the sufferer in a taxi and take her to the house of a woman friend who happened to live within a hundred yards of this place. And my little friend remained as if poisoned for the greater part of the day and did not eat breakfast, did not go to her office. It was an example of the risks of speakeasy life—speak easy and die badly!

The speakeasies are a remarkable feature of the new American life. Every time you go for a drink there is adventure. I suppose it adds to one's pleasure to change into a pirate or a dark character entering a smuggler's cave. You go to a locked and chained door. Eyes are considering you through peep-holes in the wooden walls. There is such a to-do about letting you in. Some one for the first time must be sponsor. You sign your name in a book and receive a mysterious-looking card with only a number on it. The bartender says to you suggestively as you sign your name, "And you will please *remember* your address." And you are admitted to a back-parlour bar with a long row of stooping and loquacious drinkers. There may be only three bottles in use, the main supply being hidden away in some place less liable to raids. There may be a red signal light which can be operated from the door in case of revenue officer or police demanding entrance, and at the red light signal the contents of the three bottles are incontinently emptied into the street below.

At the men's bars there seems to be more nervousness and drama than at the fashionable mixed saloons. At one bar named after a flower which opens its cups at night the whole drinking company were requested to go out at about two one morning just for half an hour because the stairway was infested by suspicious-looking characters who demanded to be let in and would not go away. "I can't take no chances, gentlemen," said the bartender. "I've just got to close up for a while." "Open again at two-thirty maybe."

I had some amusing adventures with men who volunteered to take me a round of the bar-rooms. But they were generally cut short by the incapacity of the guides. Synthetic whisky sets a man on and then very quickly sets him off, "it makes him stand to, and not stand to" as the porter says in Macbeth.

"Excuse me, I'm so drunk I can't walk across Broadway," said one. "Put me in a cab and let's call it a night."

But in New York I did not call anything a night that ended before midnight.

I made a jolly round with one of the oldest of New York reporters, a man who had been out every night for the last thirty years, now attached to the Station House of the White Light district. His was decidedly a seasoned head. With every glass of "inspiration" he took two chasers of beer.

"Mine's inspiration please," he said each time, that being bar-slang for rye.

He lasted till three in the morning.

The lights of the Great White Way are like the shop lanterns of hundreds of bars. All around that circle of theatrical glare are the quiet alley-ways and entrances of drinking places. The police are not concerned to close them, indeed they will direct you to them. At one of them I met a couple of detectives who were drinking beer and finishing their pencil notes on a burglary they had been investigating. It was only a few doors up from the police station though separated by a Catholic church and a synagogue.

Every bar has its peculiarity. This one had interlocking doors. When you entered one door the inner automatically closed. When the bar-tender opened the inner door his action closed the outer door.

At another bar which had an illuminated door of frosted glass the signal was to place an extended palm on the door, and when that shadow of a hand was seen from within the bolts were withdrawn.

One that we entered was kept by an Irishman. He has always been in the business, and preserved from his old legitimate bar a block of dry Leitrim mud which he had brought with him from Ireland thirty years before. It reposed in honour on the cash register and was tied round with emerald ribbons. The Irish are great people for keeping up the traditions.

Several bars had grills and cooked a supper. Others had free sandwich counters where you helped yourself. Others had little restaurant rooms. One, kept by a pyramidal-shaped and jovial Italian had *cabinets particuliers* where you could take your girl. The cabinets were just shuttered apartments of green painted wood—not very secret; for one saw the women's faces frequently through half-opened doors.

"You Irish?" I asked of the man behind the bar.

"No, just a plain ordinary Wop," he answered.

This was a well-known theatrical speakeasy, frequented by actors, supers, stage-hands, and what not, very democratic. Not far away is a shop which keeps open all night and displays in its windows such unusual wares as eyebrow pencils, nose putty, eye-shadow, and moist rouge. At the bar were one or two characters from the underworld of Broadway theatrical life. One debauched-looking fellow offered to show me sights that would skin my eyeballs. But my companion dismissed him as a bar-room hanger-on. "He knows nothing but bars. You ought to get a 'Graphic' reporter to take you round if you want initiation." He looked at me quizzically. "No, you don't even need a 'Graphic' reporter I guess. You'll find your way about this old town without much help."

The reporter was a little unsteady. "I was well spanked before you came along," he explained. He invited me to come with him to the Station House. There he was well known and was good friends with every one. "Officer, I want you to meet Mr. Graham; he's an ole friend, met on the other side years and years ago. 'S come to give the once over to this lan' of liberty. And when I think the 'World' newspaper raised the money to buy the pedestal to put up that dam' lie in our harbour I say the Press of this country is doing the country no good. No objection to Mr. Graham visiting your cells? Come along."

We passed a shelf crowded with liquor bottles, raided some time or other by the police, probably now containing little to drink, and went down to the basement of the building where were a number of cold stone cells with lattice-work iron doors. Here two melancholy drunks were confined. One of them, all in tears, told us how he had come to the station and requested to be locked up so as to give peace to his wife and daughter.

"My wife is very ill, but I've been raising hell all night, and I thought the only thing to do was to get locked up and give her a quiet night," said he.

We passed him through some cigarettes, and my companion, holding the iron bars and swaying, gave him a lecture on the evils of alcoholism.

"You ought to quit drinking, m' boy, before it's too late. It's poison. One day you'll be found dead in the street. Obey the laws of the country, m' boy. They're for your protection. Sure! Uncle Sam doesn't want you to get in this horrible state, a disgrace and a menace to a decent family. See? Am I right? Am I right?"

The police laughed very much at this for my companion was himself drunk and was trying to keep his balance as he gave forth this homily.

He laughed also and tottered up the stairs into the Station Hall.

Then we went to a Beauty Parlour much patronised by chorus girls and dancers from the revues. It's a very successful establishment combining two businesses, for at the back of the parlour there is a little window out of which ever and anon comes a hairy hand dispensing creature comforts to the fair unseen. A nice place! A girl goes for a manicure and gets a nip, goes for a wave and gets a splash.

In the old days in New York there were definite hours for drinking. And in London there are certain hours. But many of the bars in New York keep open all night. The new trade is very irresponsible.

One bar-tender was reproaching Scotland with getting rich by poisoning America. I said the whisky he sold never came from Scotland. It must be made locally. He said I was right.

"We get it now in the mash," he said. "And it's turned over to the guys on Eighth and Ninth Avenues to be worked up into the real stuff. God knows what they do to it. Our rye is cut many times over. There's no check on the makers. None of them ever gets charged with manslaughter. One of our members was found dead in a hotel last week with our card on him, and the police came to me to identify him. His girl had canned him and he came to us to forget it, drank too much, and died of it. They brought it in 'suicide through strychnine poisoning.'

"But we're dropping the card system all around Broadway. You've got to get in on your face. Cards seem to be dangerous. So many get sore at us after cleaning themselves out, and they mail the card to the police with our address. The police notify us of a coming raid. But it costs us heavy. And there's not such a lot of profit in a speakeasy. Not so much as you might think with drinks at fifty cents. If you want to see where money is being made you must go to a fancy joint. It's the hostesses who sell the stuff and boost up the takings."

It was three in the morning. Some one looking at my companion winked knowingly, and a jovial Irishman behind the bar began to lie—

"All out, boys; going to close now. All out, boys."

He thought the reporter had reached that stage when it was better to go home.

"May the Lord God give rest to all peaceful souls," chanted an Irish bar-tender goodnaturedly. "All out, boys."

And a young fellow took my companion by the arm and led him to the door and dexterously ejected him. I followed and took his arm, leading him laboriously to the subway.

Wherever I went in New York, be it the journalists' booth at Police Headquarters, or a fashionable tea, or a convivial dinner at a friend's house, or a night club, or a publisher's office, friends and acquaintances, the intimate or the chance met, whispered addresses to me which I scribbled in my note-book, addresses and pass words. There came to be so many that I forgot who gave me each.

The clientele of one place I visited grew like a snowball. I was taken by a New York editor, and he inscribed my name in the proprietor's book. Next day I took a friend and inscribed his name. But you could not get in till your name had been written down.

One night I chose a place at random from my notebook list. It was on West Forty-sixth Street. I had to give the name of S. K. I took a friend. The taxi put us down opposite a very dark and gloomy-looking house. The basement had an iron gateway like the entrance to a prison. "This place has been raided and closed," I said to my companion, and felt disappointed, but upon ringing the bell a man with a head shaped like an egg came from an interior door and parleyed through the gate.

"Who are you?"

"I am S. K."

"Are you sure?"

"Yes, that is the name."

"I don't recognize you."

He went and brought the boss.

"You S. K.?" he queried.

"That's right."

The boss, a florid Italian, hesitated dramatically, and then took a chance and bade us be admitted.

We had dinner and were very adequately served, though plied with expensive drinks. But there was an interruption.

The man with head like an egg returned and queried:

"Are you sure you are S. K.?"

"That was the name given me."

"But you are not S. K. himself?"

"No."

"Because S. K. is in the kitchen. Perhaps he is a friend of yours."

"I will go see him. He is probably a literary man."

But the real S. K. was a stockbroker and he glared at me. I explained very sweetly that I was a literary man exploring New York at night, and he was mollified by that.

When I came to pay my bill the boss poured forth a *douceur* for my companion and myself—

two glasses of real apricot brandy. "I'd take it as a favour," he said, "if you are writing about New York, not to mention my place."

"Certainly," I promised. "I name no place and compromise none. Good night."

At another resort of this kind my bill was discharged by the boss—on condition that I did not mention his establishment. Amusing this, in New York, where normally there is such a craving for publicity.

I was told that I was leading a life of danger, going the rounds of the speakeasies. I ought to take out a heavy life-insurance. I have no doubt it was so, especially as I am an abstemious person and have no particular pleasure in drinking spirits. But I survived in good health. Perhaps that was due to the walks I had between three in the morning and dawn. It is exhilarating to walk the empty streets of the great city and for me, despite my amused interest in the ways of speakeasies, I was happier outside than inside.

CHAPTER VI

At Romany Marie's

UP a narrow stairway and past a stout coloured cook filling a little kitchen, past a long line of free hat pegs hung with coats of visitors, are two rooms, shadowy, ornate, reposeful, and at some tables people are playing chess, at others people are talking in low voices, at others people are watching a Japanese sketching with tiny brush and Indian ink. Suddenly the café is mildly aroused, for one of the groups has become strangely vocal. A plaintive and shrill voice is singing an Asiatic song which is out of keeping with the spirit of New York. A new instrument has introduced a new *motif* and one divines that the orchestra turns to a new theme. A short thickset man comes out of the shadow toward me, a drab figure with red face and small light blue eyes. It is Steffanson the explorer whom I have not seen in an age. He comes tip-toeing toward me, as he were on the tight rope of a Northern meridian, with Eskimo music behind him and the shadow flicker and red glimmer of the aurora showing his face.

The singer is Therese du Gautier, who has been in Northern Canada collecting Eskimo music. With her is the French musician Edgar Varese. Her chant is an Eskimo lullaby sung before New York was, and no doubt to be sung after it has gone. The scene is Romany Marie's garret in Washington Square. An unearthly keening, snow-huts, little people fur-wrapped, reindeer, darkness dimly lighted by snow, explorers, an explorer's mind— A spell has been wrought. But what does it mean? Where am I? Whose goloshes have I put on by mistake?

The green 'buses roll down Fifth Avenue into the Square, like the weights of wall-clocks, self-winding, keeping the whole city ticking. Washington Square is the kitchen floor of New York in which a tall grandfather's clock is ticking, steadily ticking—"Forever Never: Never Forever. As 'Twas so 'Twill be. As 'Twill be so 'Twas." It registers, registers—what does it register? Time, heart beats, civilisation, history? The wail of the Eskimo music seems to remind us that it is not civilisation. It says so much that is paradoxical, says that the West is East, that the New World is the Old World. Asia seems to expand in the night, Europe is an extension of Asia, America an extension of Europe. In an occult sense Asia is the subconsciousness of every one, Asia is the world.

The singer becomes silent. There is quietude in the low-roofed night club. Some one pokes the embers of the log fire and miniature meteors fly up the vent, sparks and smoke with a subsidence of grey ash. People are whispering—the Japanese, unperturbed, goes on sketching, the chess players stare at their locked wooden battles. Romany Marie floats up to Therese du Gautier with coffee and congratulations.

Congratulations always seem irrelevant after a

miracle. Romany Marie, stout, swarthy, empearled, with crimson ribbon in her black hair and peasant art evident in her embroidered dress, is a Jewess bearing the protective colouring of a Rumanian. To take part in the disenchantment of New York one ought not to be a Hebrew. Israel and business are too much identified. Be a Rumanian! Be a Gipsy!

"I was born in an inn on the fringe of a great forest in Moldavia," says Marie. "My mother kept the inn. She met my father first in the depths of the forest. He had a red kerchief about his neck; he was wild-eyed; he was full of song." Once, far, far away from here between Rumania and Bessarabia there was a wayside inn on the edge of a dark forest. That forest stretched away to the Dneister and the Ukraine, without a break. In it there wandered many gipsy bands. It was quite like the beginning of a fairy tale.

"I am one of a wandering tribe loving freedom and song; that is why I am so glad when travellers come to the garret, yourself, Steffanson, George Brown the Scotch gipsy. When I was on Christopher Street all the Bohemians came to me. They talk about me in Paris, in Budapest, in Vienna. They all know Romany Marie's. Picasseau has painted here. O'Neill wrote some of his plays sitting before my fire."

Like a living visitor's book Romany Marie recalled the visit of the Prince of Wales. Every American loves the Prince of Wales' feathers.

Faces, faces, faces, and among them that of the debonair, cosmopolitan, amusing Prince, with its mechanical smile. Yes, he is a traveller, a sort of royal gipsy, a child stolen by the gipsies to be returned later on to a throne.

"Guido Bruno used to live here once and he edited his weekly from this studio," Romany Marie continued, striving unnecessarily to make her garret memorable to me. At Steffanson's suggestion Mlle. du Gautier had begun to sing another Eskimo song, one specially dear to him. He had heard her sing it several times. So had Edgar Varese. But they wished it repeated. There were elusive unheard-of quarter tones in it. It was music that had no reference to music. We were stilled and listened. Marie went away silently to the kitchen. The Japanese with studious interested eyebrows went on sketching, his face softened with musical reserves and unspoken thoughts. The Oriental has a commoner habit of communing with his soul than we have. We marvel outwardly; the Easterns marvel inwardly. So the spell was re-imposed. Washington Square faded out. The foundations of Fifth Avenue rocked. Where millions were cooped together there was just one voice quavering and shrilling out of the primeval wilderness of man's heart.

The rugged Norwegian Steffanson is a rock-like person, unemotional, hard, like most Norwegians. He seemed to grow harder, more compact, as he listened, as if a rock could edify. Varese was different. He is a modern French musician of the type of Stravinsky, not eschewing the cacophonies, the discordant and elusive; not traditional, extra-traditional. One felt his active attention, not merely receptive but creative. The rest of us were merely muted and rendered inoperative by the musical negatives coming upon our ears.

It was different when the Frenchwoman turned to Canadian-French folk-music. We were rendered more comfortable, were nearer together, more domestic. The centuries telescoped and gentle Europe consoled the spirit with its communicable hopes and loves. The old pots on the shelves, the country plates on the walls, were pleased. We had been taken in out of the wilderness to a peasant's cottage. Somewhere there was a *pot-au-feu*.

It was not even a wayside inn in Moldavia. It was old France, pre-revolution, France under a Louis, obscure and simple. The Aurora Borealis flashed no more, the hungry stars dimmed out, to a roof of smoke and thatch. The soul had changed rooms in the universe which is outside New York —below, behind it, and around it.

CHAPTER VII

At Texas Guinan's

ONE thing that has charmed me in America is the spirit of co-operation. You have only to announce your intention of studying some aspect of the national life, and America comes forth to help you. It is like the fairy-tale when the boy setting forth on his quest of treasure is met at each corner of the road by some mysterious helper. When arriving in New York I knew nothing of the night life I was going to study and therefore was as unlikely as any hero of a fairy-tale. On the boat I was actually told that there was no night life: Prohibition had killed it. I thought then that it would be interesting describing New York asleep at ten-thirty. I would write a short study entitled "Curfew in New York."

London thinks of New York as very lively, but it knows nothing of Texas Guinan's, or Barney Galant's or the Paradise Club. Florence Mills in her show of "Blackbirds" has a scene presenting "The Nest," but who has heard of that charming night club outside of New York? Van Vechten's "Nigger Heaven" awakened a mild curiosity regarding Harlem but not one in ten thousand Englishmen knows whether Harlem is a district, or a city, or a cabaret. And the average Englishman arriving in New York depends on his hosts rather than on himself for his entertainment. How differently the same man would arrive in Paris, intent on a gay time and knowing quite explicitly

TEXAS GUINAN
This little girl invites you to give her a hand.

what he intended to do and where he intended to go! I had not heard of Texas Guinan's in London except as a name associated with records of the music of her orchestra. And when I heard an American say, "Because you call Texas Guinan by her first name, don't think you won the war," I did not understand the reference. Then in the first days in New York a lounger in a theatrical speakeasy said, "You're studying night life. Give me two hundred bucks and I'll take you to Texas Guinan's. It all starts there." I did not part with the two hundred bucks but I was interested in the striking name. I met William Beebe, the hero of the Arcturus, one who not only knows life down-under in the ocean but down-under in the ocean of New York. He is a brilliant star-like person who looks at you, as it were from an eye in the centre of his fine brow. He also impressed on me the advantage of seeing Texas soon, and he called her the most wonderful mixer of the Bohemian elements of New York Society to-day.

The general impression I obtained was that a ticket for the Three Hundred Club,* as Texas Guinan's was then politely called, being a club for the original four hundred less the hundred undesirables, was equivalent to the "freedom of the city by night." "Jimmy Walker rules New York by day; Texas Guinan by night." It was not all that perhaps, but it was an important door.

My first night at the Three Hundred Club re-

* Subsequently padlocked and reopened as the 48th Street Club.

mains memorable. I came at midnight, and at seven in the morning I was still there sitting at a table with Texas, Harry Thaw, a bedizened Frenchwoman called Fifi, handsome Bill B— a screen star, and a young angel-millionaire who at that hour in the proceedings seemed pathetically in love with old man Guinan's daughter and forgetful of all else in the world. There were others, yes, but it was the end of the festivity. Most of the guests had gone home and Texas herself was eating cantaloupe and chicken sandwiches surrounded by her retainers, and discoursing in her large voice of the triumphs of the night and of triumphs to be.

The room is long, but not too long to be homely. No one can be lost in it. The walls are covered with pleated cloth and the roof tented with the same cloth softly toned in old rose, green, and sere yellow. There are hanging Chinese lanterns, and on the walls illuminated designs of parrots. There are twenty or thirty tables and a small space in the middle of them for intimate dancing.

The lighting is wonderful. There is nothing to try the eyes or irritate one. It is radiantly lighted and yet it is not the light associated with noisy excitement and jazz. You have come there not for a giddy hour but for hours and hours. That is why the illumination is so carefully toned. You part with your hat and coat; you are conducted to a table and you realise the pleasure of an intimate companion with whom you can talk of the things of the heart for three or four hours, punctuating your conversation with dancing.

A charming girl in blue satin trousers and wearing a crimson sash comes offering cigarettes, arriving at each table like a blown wisp of silk or a moth to a flower. This is Ethel, equally elegant and fresh at each hour of the night. Alternating with her is a smart girl in black with silver flowers on her hips, carrying large ornate dolls which indulgent New Yorker male likes to buy for his lady friend. He gives his "baby" a baby, his "cutie" a cutie, his "baby-doll" a baby-doll. It is a sort of playful identification. Or it is a symbol of the primitive interest of a man and a woman bathed in the love atmosphere. The silver-spangled nymph is a young goddess with babes for sale.

There is a low buzz of conversation. Waiters in red-faced uniforms flutter to and fro with silver-topped bottles and elaborately prepared sandwiches. Four guitarists, the "Castillians," go from table to table and play to the various parties in turn, as it were playing them in and welcoming them. They play, and then they break into rich subdued vocal harmony. They are dark men of differing heights and proportions, South Americans, romantic of feature. Each looks like a lover—a serenader under his mistress's window. They play deliberately, quietly, with subdued passion. It is a murmuring of the strings. Their steps also, as they move from one table to the next, are measured, deliberate, gracious. They remind me of the preliminaries at an Orthodox Mass, when incense in a processional way is carried to each of many altars. They sing gipsy songs, Spanish serenades, American ballads. They sing by request what they are asked. Their musical attentions are indulgent, the Club's personal compliment to each party of guests.

But Texas Guinan is not here. I surmise that she is still sleeping off the effects of the night before. Rumour has it she generally gets up to dinner. But one waiter says that she has looked in at her brother-in-law's night club—Tommy Guinan's. Another avers she has been to a theatre and went on to "Sherry's." The guests are expectant of her appearance and keep looking to the door. But Texas seldom arrives before one in the morning. To pass the time the band slips indolently into jazz, and the partnered crowd toes the parquet between the tables.

Some guests are leaving but new ones are arriving. The club has been open since ten-thirty. There are still some free tables. But by one o'clock there is not a free place. The room is full. Lady Diana has arrived accompanied by a Judge's son. Two famous baseball players arrive. Here comes a rich Park Avenue hostess. Here comes the wife of one of the richest bankers in America. Here comes a well-known editor whose wife thinks he is pounding out editorials on world affairs, and instead he has a fascinating blonde on his arm.

Here comes Don Rafael, a wealthy Spaniard who has the torso of a bull-fighter and the assurance of one of the three musketeers. I see the Mayor flitting in elegantly to touch the hands of several of a large party and yield his charming smile to the ladies.

As I look at the square bottles on the tables my mind goes back to a verse on the London Underground trains:—

> "From Underground to everywhere
> Matured by age and bottled square."

and I wonder if Mayor Walker of New York has any connection with famous Johnny Walker.

Many guests seem to bring bottles with them, and I am afraid these took away from sartorial grace. Even the smallest flask rather disfigures a Tuxedo. It seems appalling for rich and elegant males to dance with bottles in their pockets. Ladies of course have to risk leaving their bottles on the tables, but it was sad to see one of the most beautiful women exquisitely dressed yet pressing a big bottle of whisky to her bosom under her shawl of Persian silk.

In the midst of all this was one octogenarian lady with white hair and one child of thirteen who danced with her tall father.

"Look, the dancing grandmother has come," said my neighbour, pointing to the old lady. "You should see her dance. She's full of passion."

I did not know Texas by sight. But at half past

one she arrived and was unmistakable. No stranger needed to ask who was Texas Guinan. There she was like a queen, like the sun, like a big firework, like a gorgeous tamer who has just let herself into a large cage of pet tigers. The name was whispered from table to table, Texas, Texas.

She is a big woman, buxom to say the least. Of any age, with the grace of twenty-five. Her father is seventy. But you do not think of her age. She has a sort of immortal look. She was clad in a rose-coloured dress with cream lace gorget and the same lace low down her back. There was an enormous rose on her right shoulder lying on a large leaf. Her thick blond hair was rigidly waved. She wore a triple necklet of large pearls, and two ropes of pearls from her shoulders to her waist, and she had rose-coloured slippers with sparkling rhinestone heels. There was a large pearl in a ring on one of her fingers. A woman of considerable physical strength and good carriage. She walked well and with assurance.

A kiss here, a stroke of the hand there, an uttered "darling" there, she went from table to table clasping the company into a unity about her personality. Her smile seemed to be very prepossessing, a very magnetic winning smile. When I went up to her to introduce myself I am sure she had not the remotest idea who I was or why I had come, but she smiled in a royal way which Queen Victoria could not have bettered, promising to come to my table presently; "I want to have a talk with you," she said.

More kisses, young men came up to her and demanded personal caresses. "Hello, Corrie; hello, Harry, Jimmy, Charlie. Hello, Charlie, I see your old flame is on the other side of the room. Well, Diana! Isn't this Rafael my beau? Say, Harry, where's your wife—do you still love her? I'm so glad."

She spoke in a deep voice, not with her lips but with her whole body. There was no mistaking her voice. It rose over the other sounds in the room. However, she was later than usual in arriving and wanted to get the show started. One of her handsome cavaliers helped her and she climbed on to a chair. She stroked his head in thanks, and then, erect and magnificent, began to boss the company, the band, the waiters, and the dancers.

Click-clacks of painted wood were on most of the tables, but Texas had a heap of them handed up to her and she served catches to men and women all over the room. Sure as she caught your eye she hurled you a clapping machine. Her roseate form erect there in the midst of the company kept the whole interest in herself, and by throwing the clappers she kept the gaze of all and sundry jumping to her.

The near-naked girls came out and sang a song about cherries. One carried a basket of fruit. She sang very attractively, and at the chorus, "Cherries! Cherries!" all the waiters shouted "Cherries!" All the guests shouted "Cherries!" The whole room resounded with hoarse cries as if it had become a fruit market, "Cherries!" "Cherries!" Texas encouraged the whole staff to be noisy, her idea now being to get every one excited. The girl with the basket made the tour of the tables and put a cherry into each man's mouth. One took the cherry and kissed the girl's finger-tips. A girl following ruffled up men's hair as she passed. Great fun having your hair ruffled by a kid! It made the young men feel like fathers. A new profession for girls—hair-rufflers!

Texas all the while kept throwing clappers and making loud remarks to new friends as more and more visitors crowded in. A troupe of girl sprites from the back got hold of one young fellow, pulled him to bits, lugging off his coat, unbuttoning his vest, handing up to Texas his watch, his pocket-book, and the rest of the contents of his pockets. He seemed to enjoy it immensely, and while he dressed again the girl sprites in a ring danced round him. Then he encircled the waists of one or two of them and smacked them and got away.

There was a succession of young dancers, white girls whose glimmering bodies so near and intimate produced not merely an *odeur des femmes*. Adam ceased to be interested by the garden and was only interested in his rib. It was merely the show-off of pretty girls, "fair and pleasant for delights."

Russian ballet would have been out of place, too intellectual and æsthetic. For the ballet, like all true dancing, is art. But this was indulgence, a picnic without a wood, in an artificial summer. But it was light-hearted and gay, not like the atmosphere of burlesque, or of the Folies Bergères or Moulin Rouge. Texas Guinan has the art to make her party young—gay, light-hearted, irresponsible.

As in a burlesque of Vachel Lindsay's recitations, the audience was continually called upon to shout some line in the midst of the songs. A girl knowingly points to her two eyes and two breasts and sings "She has this and she has that." And the crowd, or in any case the waiters, interrupt in chorus with the line *"And she knows her onions."*

Texas, with an air of kindness, kept calling on the audience to applaud new singers and dancers. "Oh, encourage that girl. Give that little girl a hand!" she would implore, suiting the action to the word by shaking her click-clack noisily, and thus she would obtain a chorus of applause.

During the songs the waiters amused themselves by shouting, "Louder, louder!" "Louder and funnier!"

"Sonya, Sonya!" (This to a Russian dancer.)

"Gigolo, Gigolo!"

"O. K. O. K."

"All right, Texas! All right, Texas!"

They seemed to me rather out of hand. But the hostess herself encouraged this and I suppose knew what she was about. The clamour helped to unify the crowd of guests.

The revue culminated in a snow-ball fight. Scores of felt snow-balls were brought in baskets and distributed among the guests. Every one began to throw balls at the man and woman of his particular fancy. White balls flew in all directions in the rosy light of the Chinese lanterns, responsive laughter bubbling up from all quarters. Lady Diana put her pretty head in an inverted basket to save it from being pelted.

After this sham battle the jazz band resumed its musical invitation, and there was general dancing. Even Texas, somewhat unwillingly, was captured by a gallant partner and led round.

I had an interesting talk with her father—"Old Man Guinan," as the staff familiarly call him. He was originally British, belonging to a Dublin Irish family which settled in Canada. His daughter's real name is Marie Louise, named after the Princess. But the father made home and fortune in Texas. The daughter who before she was an impresario was a cinema star and before that a Texan cow-girl, did well to be known as Texas, "fair as a star when only one is shining in the sky." She can rope steers as ably as she can rope dancers, and at times her club has something of the rodeo in the air.

"My daughter is a born mixer, and she's full of pep and good-humour and everything else," said he. "Wherever she goes she makes friends. President Harding adored her. Mrs. Harding not less. She and the Prince of Wales were the best of friends."

The old man is a character derived you might say direct from Thackeray, and I can imagine how that master hand would have dealt with him and his daughter in a novel.

He's a delightful old fellow who doesn't care a rap for the conventions. After an adventurous life in business speculation and finance he is now his daughter's manager and runs the commercial side. Not that Texas herself is not shrewd enough to do that better than he can at his age but, being out all the night she must be free of the day.

Mr. Guinan told me of the millions he had won and of the millions he had lost, the corner he had made in seed potatoes, the hold he had had on vast numbers of priority railroad shares, the fights he had had with railroad kings, and of the wonderful deal he nearly concluded with the Harding administration, and if half of it was not exaggerated some one ought to be at pains to write his biography. Texas gave Harding so great pleasure and he so admired her that he sent for the old man and desired to know in what way he might advance him in honour and estate, to show his gratitude.

"Tell me what I can do for you, socially, commercially, financially."

The old man said he would like to help his country by cutting the prices on certain Government contracts by twenty-five per cent.

"No," said the President, "you should have control of these contracts, and if there is a margin of twenty-five per cent, why, I think it only fair that you should benefit."

"I placed an order that night for nine billion envelopes," said Mr. Guinan. "All was drawn up and was waiting to be signed. Mr. Harding took the document away with him. But a great personal and national misfortune intervened. The President never came back."

"When did you become an American citizen?" I asked him.

"In 1878 when I came to Texas. Exactly two hours and fifteen minutes after I arrived I forsook Queen Victoria and recorded my vote for the Democratic ticket. But I have always retained the greatest respect for the British Empire, its laws and its administration, and would rather be governed under British law than under United States."

But this remark was partly compliment to me and partly irritation at the liquor laws. Great Britain is frightfully popular at bars and in night clubs in New York.

Between the hours of three and five in the morning almost half the company at the club paid their bills and left. But other visitors flocked in to take their places. The ordinary clubs of the White Light district close between three and four, and numbers of their guests came along to look up Texas. They were mostly lit up with pleasure before they arrived. Some revue girls with partners came in. A popular actor hailed as Eddie appeared. Harry Thaw, who had perhaps been there all night, emerged into view and I was able to consider his very extraordinary face. Don Rafael became very prominent. Handsome and adored Charlie, Charlie what, I don't know, began to receive many attentions from Texas and from the other ladies.

There was to be a second revue at five o'clock, and Texas was busily engaged restraining those who thought of home and bed and in welcoming newcomers. She held several departing guests by sheer force of will. She appeared to be in excellent spirits, and hit men over the head with her clapper as she passed them. A lately-married couple fresh from their honeymoon appeared. "Oh-ho, the newlyweds!" she cried, and sent a waiter for a bag of rice. Every now and then she caught my eye and fixed me. "Don't go!" I had told her I might describe the night in a book, and she appeared very eager that I should have a full impression. "Don't go, Diana, don't go," she cried, seeing that lady show signs of making a move. "The second show is beginning."

Texas used all sorts of devices to delay the going of those who had risen, and she was often successful. She had great power of will, and I marvelled at her energy, and vitality.

The five o'clock revue was pleasant. There were not quite so many people. Texas, after a bout of pelting the newlyweds with rice, settled down at a long table to enjoy the show herself, her admirers clustered about her. Her table would have made an excellent movie picture, for there was a great deal of facial expression and the group was unified by the dominant personality of Texas herself.

When she wanted the lights low she called "Cohen!" and all the waiters shouted "Cohen!" The lights were low during most of the second revue. I noticed that some of the guests were asleep in their seats. One of the waiters borrowed a horn from the jazz band and blew dreadful reveilles into the ears of the sleepers. But they did not awake. Bootleg sleep is most profound. Some one whispered to me that there was a special tariff for those who could not be awakened by a trumpet. Some guests looked as if Gabriel himself could not have disturbed them.

I had grown accustomed to being out all night, but I began to feel tired. There were a number of tired and faded but hypnotised people there. Some were irritable, and I foresaw the chance of some one starting a fight in the club. But a charming girl in a cerise coat and ninon knickers crooned "Baby face! Baby face!" And a score sang it with her. And a trio of young girls in Oxford trousers sat in chairs in the rosy twilight and sang "Blackbird" sweetly, indulgently, pathetically—

> Make my bed and light the light,
> I'll be home late to-night.

As it neared six o'clock in the morning these words began to seem without meaning. But I gathered that many of those present were at Texas Guinan's night after night, all night. The ordinary sweetness of darkness and night meant nothing to them; they defied it, denied it. If they slept with their wives they slept by day. Still, all were affected with "Bye-bye, blackbird" sentimentality. Even Texas with her tireless bursting energy seemed stilled. The waiters standing about in the dim light looked like wax-works. The company drooped like flowers at sunset. There seemed after all to be some sadness, perhaps some tragedy hidden in the lives of these fearfully gay people.

Then the lights went up and playful nymphs emerged. Don Rafael made himself a nuisance by encircling their waists with his arm and leading them about to introduce them personally to those they already knew. He had been attempting this all night to shouts of "Sit down! Sit down!" He was making himself unpopular. Suddenly some one picked a quarrel with him and there was a scuffle in which one of the ropes of Texas' pearls got broken. Waiters intervened to part the fighters, and there was a good deal of confusion.

Harry Thaw, gabbling and laughing beside Texas, seemed monstrously amused, but she was angry and began to use threats and persuasions, commands and coaxings, to stop the feud. A real fight was narrowly averted. The Spaniard retreated in chagrin. He was in the wrong, but

Texas was fond of him and called him a "Swell feller." But the American who was accompanied by a beautiful and distinguished-looking lady she seemed also unwilling to offend.

Half a dozen men on the floor were seeking her lost pearls, to which however Texas seemed indifferent. Nowadays no one gets excited over lost pearls. But I thought the tireless good mixer might for a moment lose her self-control. She said to me, "I'm so—" She was going to say "tired," but she would not admit it.

Don Rafael, having swallowed his insult, came to say "Good-bye. Texas looked at him appealingly. "You're still my beau, always my beau." And he gravely accepted her assurance and caress.

Texas had her breakfast brought in.

"Well, Harry," she said, "are you going to give me a copy of that book of yours?"

Thaw seemed flattered, but there were two expressions on his strange face. His eyes and brow seemed in conflict with his mouth and chin.

He spoke like a turkey gobbling.

"You'll buy a copy and then I'll autograph it for you . . . I'm a mean fellow, I am."

"Bill, you look like Jack O'Brien of Philadelphia. Quit staring at him."

The gentleman addressed was leaning forward and staring with a fixed expressionless stare.

An actor brought in Fifi.

I was next to Texas on one side, on the other was a young fellow who kept telling her in a tear-stricken voice how he loved her and asking her not to make fun of him. She said she would never make fun of him. "Let me take you home in my car. I promise you I won't hurt you," said he. As if any one could harm Texas Guinan!

At that moment Harry Thaw stood up and appeared to be about to fight the newly-come actor.

"If Harry is going to fight I'll not be a witness," cried Texas, stood up, and with Fifi suddenly made her escape and went home.

Then we all went home.

It was strange to walk out into the broad daylight from that radiant room of everlasting midnight and find it was pouring with rain and that the morning toilers were hurrying through it to their daily work.

CHAPTER VIII

At Texas Guinan's (Suite)

MY last dance in the Fall was at Texas Guinan's. Patricia and I spent the night out and were there till six-thirty in the morning of the day I sailed for England. We promised that on my first night back in America we would celebrate by going to Texas again. But much intervened during the winter. Texas Guinan's had been padlocked when I returned.

I had read something of her adventures. First, Aimée MacPherson had been to the club with another revivalist and had had a "swell time," whatever that means. I imagine it would be an act of great courage to attempt to save souls in a night club. Real apostolic fervour would be required for that, which is something rarely possessed by the revivalists. They looked in and saw that the night club was innocent and Texas was very sweet to them and that was all. They sing a witty song about it now at the new club. And Texas when a little later she was arrested by federal officers who raided the club, exclaimed as she got down from the chair where she had been standing, "I don't care, only let me have some devotional books along."

An onslaught was made on the night clubs during the winter. Many were closed and I saw the yellow padlocks on the doors of several places I used to visit. Clubs had changed their names. Jack had removed his speakeasy from 54th Street to 48th. Jack's brother had decided to extend business and was opening a new drinking establishment on top of a skyscraper. A curfew law had been promulgated by the Commissioner of Police requiring all places of amusement to close at or before three in the morning. Not that any old man goes round the streets of New York at three in the morning ringing a bell. But the police are given the opportunity to call.

Texas was not arrested by the New York police, who have always been friendly to her, but by federal agents. The Three Hundred Club was shut up. But the proceedings against the lady proved farcical. She stood up and amused the court and the judge with her witty repartees and it was decided that whatever went on in the club she was not responsible. She was nominally not the proprietor of the club but an employé. There was therefore no case against her.

Also during the winter rumour had it that Texas had been rejuvenated. As a witty journalist put it "Map of Texas Lifted." A woman I met shortly after my return, Mrs. Arbuckle, also a leading hostess of night clubs, said, "Texas is the queen of night clubs, she can never be suppressed." I felt there was something immortal about her.

So one night I espied an electric sign on 48th Street. It said "Texas Guinan and her Mob Open April 6th." Patricia and I therefore decided to keep our tryst.

I had been up to Columbia to fulfil an engagement to speak with Milt Gross on the twin topics of Humour and Being Serious before the Writers Club. It was a curious contrast coming from the quiet ladies of the faculty to the joy-cave of Texas.

We arrived about midnight when there were not many people. There were more waiters than guests. Texas had not yet come. We got a good table and surveyed the new scene. The room was smaller than that of the Three Hundred Club, but it was brighter, more playful. It had sham windows framed with illuminated coloured caricatures of New York celebrities such as Texas herself and Paul Whiteman. On strings across and across hung numerous red, yellow and blue balloons. There was a good square of dancing floor, and tables three sides of it. The same set of waiters were there, Ethel, the cigarette girl, loped indolently along. The girl who used to sell flowers was now selling magnolias. All the guests began to wear their white blossoms. She told us that Sonya the Russian girl was performing at the Loew State Theatre, "going over great."

Patricia and I danced till Texas came in. It was a very hot night but an artificial breeze such as one might feel on a boat at sea tossed the pretty coloured balloons about and wafted our faces while we moved to the music. It was as if the band was producing a gale.

Many new guests came in and presently a roar of clapping heralded Texas herself—"Texas, Texas!" I was so surprised. In came a charming young person dressed in a slight Dubarry gown, a lissom figure in spun gold. She wore the same Texas pearls and cleverly combed auburn hair. She was radiant with smiles, she carried a police whistle in one hand and blew it vociferously every two or three seconds. She moved about with an equestrian grace and the cow-girl in her was very apparent. All the waiters rattling their clappers, the band in musical uproar, balloons popping and the whistle blowing—men in all parts standing up, shouting and waving to Texas Guinan, imparted a delirious excitement to the night club, and this excitement once begun did not die down for hours. What a vitality and animal magnetism the woman possesses!

Texas went from table to table greeting her friends, breaking from each in turn by shouting some witticism. Any mark of attention was an honour. No one wanted to be overlooked by her. I felt a glow of pleasure as if I had been moved up nearer the throne when she slapped me playfully on the cheek.

Texas on her chair ruling the giddy throng, throwing clappers, streamers, snowballs, blowing her whistle, summoning her henchmen, silencing the guests for a moment, propounding a riddle:

"Who is the greatest flapper on the American stage?"

"Fanny Ward, this one, that one . . ."

"No, the greatest flapper on the American stage, I'll tell you. It's the American flag."

Texas calling out the girls for her revue and asking the guests to rattle their clappers, make a big noise for each little dancer. . . . "Come on, give this girl a hand," Texas demurely listening to a man singing a ballad about her, accompanied by four guitarists, about her conversion by Miss MacPherson, her arrest, her friendship with the Mayor, the lights all suddenly switched out, and the band firing at the balloons with toy pistols causing resounding pops, cries of "Chicago, Chicago!" one tiny light appearing making dimly lucent the hanging balloons, the night club shrouded in soft darkness while a beautifully dressed girl does an Oriental dance waving rich luminous silk about her, the lights up again, Texas blowing her whistle insistently, in the reduced noise she addresses a lively guest whom she calls California:

"I want you to say after me the words *What am I doing?*, putting the accent first on the what, then on the am, then on I, and last of all on the word doing. You will see it alters the sense."

"The answer is either a horse or a flower," replies California, who is waggishly mellow and obstinately refuses to obey Texas.

Texas whistles, whistles, whistles, insists, and California drunkenly and self-consciously repeats the words—"*What* am I doing? What *am* I doing? What am *I* doing? What am I *doing?*"

"You're making a dam' fool of yourself. Don't you see?" rejoins Texas with great mirth.

Once more much whistling. Texas calls on the waiters to eject a college-boy who won't sit down when told to by her. "Give him his check. Come on, you rascals. Show you can do something besides lift watches and diamonds from the tables. Throw him out." But every one is throwing snowballs and streamers and in the hubbub the incident is passed over. Texas dances with each of her beaus in turn. We all dance. We are pelted with snowballs while we dance. Our feet are ankle-deep in coloured paper. About our necks and our heads and our hair trails coloured paper. The wind blows the balloons about and men and women pinch them as they pass and burst them. The exuberant band plays the Kinkajou. A vast gentleman who looks like Sam Hill tries to dance that with his sweetie. Late-comers arrive dancing as they come. One of the Fairbanks twins arrives with her newly gotten husband. Texas gives a signal and the orchestra leaves off playing jazz and breaks into the wedding-march. A horn-blower goes ahead of the happy pair brazening forth joy. Musicians and guests join in a Bacchanalian procession round the room. Then once more the dancing-square is filled and we whirl to the strains of "Do, do, do what you've done, done, done, before, baby!" Curfew passes; four o'clock passes; the dawn light is coming up in the sky outside but the star of Texas does not pale. Gaiety goes on.

Patricia and I said adieu to the Queen. "Good-bye, darling! Don't be so long before you come again!"

CHAPTER IX

New Yorkers

SHAW in *Pygmalion* identified the suburban habitats of people in a crowd by the characteristic differences in their cockney accent. In New York a clever reader of faces might be able to tell at a glance on what floor a man lived. People are beginning to get a 15th floor look. Faces of mountaineers are beginning to appear in the streets of New York, uplifted, bardic. There is a great deal of difference between the depressed expressions of those who dwell on ground-floors and those who inhabit the peaks. It is a terrible burden to carry the sense of there being twenty storeys above one. The pioneers of Manhattan are up in the cerulean; these are the people with the views and the air; the people who have got out of the shadow. They go to the window and say, "Just look out at this marvellous wonderful city." Those living down below are denied these views and get a cellar expression on their faces.

"If you're passing just drop up," says a friend to me. In what other city in the world could one hear such an expression?

This is a city of glorious movement, yes, but I do not like the symptoms of paralysis that have set in with the signalling system of pinioning the traffic. It looks as if the whole of New York were smitten with rheumatoid arthritis. These bus and taxi jerks will be reflected in the soul by and by and I expect to see some very jerky babies around.

SUBWAY JAM

The "Subway Rush" is worse than the Tube in London or the Metro in Paris.

And lovers will love in that distressing way . . . rush and halt, rush and halt.

By the way, in the imbroglio of New York traffic what is the true function of the cross-town tram? I always give one a chance, if it passes me I catch it at the next halt. Generally I overtake two or three when I cross the town. They get passengers because they obstruct pedestrians and also I suppose because the new race of New Yorkers has no feet.

There seem to be scarcely any street-criers in New York. I have heard one man cry, "I cash old clothes," but that is all. I suppose the general noise has killed the voice of the hawker. And, alas, none is selling flowers in the street. There is such noise on Sixth and Third Avenues that my soft English is always misheard on those streets. I am silenced as I walk with my friend. But there is an avenue tribe which is at home in this din. The children of Third and Sixth Avenues talk two octaves higher than those of Fourth and Madison.

The means of locomotion seem too to be producing a caste system of manners. There is the subway push, the taxi flutter, the elevated airiness, the automobile poise. The subway pushers however do seem to set the pace. It is a terrible city for pushing. On the other hand, people carry themselves well. That is because they have to raise their eyes constantly to high points in the air. The skyscrapers are straightening the spines of each and all. You do not have to say to the growing boy, "Look up, boy, look up!"

The crowd has light steps. Only the police are heavily shod. So many people dance at night that the rubber-heel industry must be suffering. New York men look less elegant than they did before Prohibition. They seem more bulky about the hips. Flasks and the black bottom are making them hip-conscious.

Women dance together at the dining-dancings on Broadway but at the more fashionable resorts twi-feminine partnership is not tolerated. In the Village they dance together unashamed to a murmurous chorus of "fairies, fairies," and the Greenwich Village poet 'plains—

> "Fairyland's not far from Washington Square."

This is something not imitated in London, where it may still be a charming compliment to call a girl a fairy.

At a fashionable thé-dansant, in fact, at the Lorraine, I was interested to see men check in their waist-coats with hat and overcoat. At the Pavilion Royal an enthusiastic dancer asked a waiter for a a fresh collar. At Arcadia I saw a man with large perspiration marks on his coat. At the Pennsylvania Grill one night I saw a fat elderly inebriated couple after jostling several people fall over one another in the middle of the floor. They picked one another up ruefully, kissed and continued to try to dance.

Checking in the waist-coat seems not unreasonable at certain seasons. I have been at Paul Whiteman's on a Saturday night when the heat was on and the whole company was moist before it began to dance. In the hot weather in many places the men take off their coats as well. They wear belts but not braces, so it may be said that like Russians they dance in their blouses—a shirt by any other name! Hot weather breaks down many conventions of dress. In London even in summer one wears a cloak over evening-dress, but on Broadway on summer nights you see many men in dinner-jackets and light hats but without cloak.

America however is not only more untraditional than England but also more individualistic in fashion and manners. It is only on such occasions as the Straw Hat festa in the fall that a certain amount of mob discipline is applied to fashion.

I watched the dancing at the Pennsylvania one night and listened to Roger Wolfe Kahn's most admirable orchestra. I suppose most of the guests have their hotel bed-rooms at the back of their consciousness; but some have checked in their bags at the station and are dancing till within a few minutes of train. They are drummers from Oshkosh dancing with their New York flirts. But what bad dancing! What floor manners! It is curious that people so good in the organisation of business, who combine so well in trade should be so individualistic on side-walks and dance-floors. But this criticism does not apply to Southerners who are in New York. They are an unheeded pattern to the rest.

The foreign elements in New York make it rough. The Italian element is especially very burly. They take more liberties with conventions than any one. You may upon occasion see an Italian serving a soda-bar on Mulberry Bend in his B. V. D.'s. The Italians rush the traffic signals more than the other races. And they are becoming more wealthy and more prominent. "The English, the Irish, the Scotch and the Goimans is all right," says the woman who cleans my apartment, "but the Italians is gone way up since Prohibition. Won't speak to you no more; has their cars and all that. It doesn't seem fair."

The successful Italian bootleggers are too showy to please their neighbours, but I believe they have very little social ambition. The Jews are very different. They want to climb. For instance, Moskowitz told me he thought of going to England in the hope that he would be invited to play his dulcimer to the King. In all seriousness. He would be even a greater light on the East Side than he is if he could say he had played to the King of England.

New Yorkers type their love letters. I met Browne of "This Believing World," and Raphaelson of "The Jazz Singer," at Moskowitz's one night, I remember we had a lively talk about love, religion and night-life. Apropos of typing love letters, Raphaelson remarked, "They dictate them;

they keep carbon copies and they sign them—*Dictated but not read.*"

Patricia said to me one night that America had become to such an extent germ-proof and sterilised that naïve love was now almost unknown. Sophisticated is one of the commonest words of everyday speech. I heard a girl say, "I am very sophisticated intellectually. He only threw me over when he found I was not sophisticated physically." A noun has been invented. They talk of "sophisticates." The American colleges are turning out swarms of sophisticates. Those who pet in night clubs are not experiencing love's young dream; they are sophisticates.

Another word competes with sophisticated; it is synthetic. Synthetic runs sophisticated very close. It is a Prohibition word and no doubt owes its origin to "synthetic gin." Elmer Gantry is synthetic; New York is synthetic; milk is synthetic; emotions are synthetic; articles must be synthetic. A man talks to me of a new night club which will be synthetic village. In England "mixing them" is cricket slang and refers to the varying of pace in the balls of an over; but in America it means drinks. The cocktail is a figure of life. New Yorkers wilfully mix their emotions in order to get a greater "kick" out of them. Broadway dramas are put up from known ingredients, more or less skilfully mixed, mystery, terror, humour, sex, sentiment. A good story is one in which these are well mixed. The experienced person holds up his glass to the light and after sipping its contents tells you what he thinks there is in it. Nothing comes straight from God; everything comes out of coloured bottles.

I met a writer of popular science one day. He is a man who believes all things and yet is a pessimist. As a writer he is extremely successful. His mind is founded on a belief in science popularly understood. But he seems to be disillusioned about life. You cannot mix him anything for which he will not give you the formula. "What next in writing?" was a question which he propounded to me. I said, "Why not compile a book of unanswerable questions as a set-off to the present 'ask me another' craze? Americans are getting the dangerous idea that all questions can be answered." But the scientist remarked, "Yes, we *are* beginning to know a little more about everything."

Travel, gaiety, new experience seemed to have little lure left for him. The night-life which I described to him he dismissed as "carnal." I said, "What you need to do is sell all that you have and give it to the poor. Clothe yourself in rags and set off for some place like Mecca."

"Oh, I've tried it. I've tried it," said he.

But he had a charming room at the Algonquin.

I imagine that if the Gospel were rewritten for Americans with synthetic souls a story of that kind would be told. The answer to the young man. "One thing thou needest. Sell what thou hast, give it to the poor, take up thy Cross and follow me." And the answer—"I've tried it, I've tried it."

I sat next to Mrs. Tom Lamont at a dinner given in honour of Masefield at the Brevoort one night.

"What do you do at night clubs at five in the morning?" she asked me.

"You put your arm round your companion and at least imagine you are in love," I replied.

"I think there is only one person in the world I could sit up all night with," said the banker's wife.

"Your husband?"

"I was thinking of God. Do you think I could find God in a night club?"

"I think you find Him in unexpected places. You often fail to find Him in churches and religious books."

"Yes? And how about the devil?"

"I think you find God and the devil very close to one another. You stand a very fair chance of having a religious experience in a night club if your soul is due to have one."

That conversation took place before Aimée MacPherson visited Texas Guinan's.

I was invited to tea one evening by Clement Wood and Gloria Goddard, poetic tea in the "Village" which implies cocktails and shaded lights. A feature of this kind of tea is that no tea is provided.

Clement Wood with wonderful voice sang Negro spirituals; Gloria said a poem of hers about the "uxorious sycamore," clever phrase suggesting to the talkers of harems of birches, bachelor pines, shimmying aspens and other amusing combinations. One of the guests was Laura, who read a ballad which was so frightful that no one would express an opinion till I had said what I thought.

I decided to risk her enmity.

"My dear, it's terrible," said I.

Laura was not abashed. That was her own private thought. She came over and sat by me.

"And how do you find New York?" asked Laura. I said it would be very pleasant if the liquor were not so bad.

"What!" she exclaimed in dismay, "you do not like our liquor? Why, it's much better in New York than anywhere else in the world."

"Your patriotism is going too far," said I. "Lately I had some Benedictine from a bottle with 'Benedictine' on its seal, and labelled D. O. M., but having a sort of poison within. It was nearer blasphemy than boot-legging."

"But, Mr. Graham, you can get wonderful Benedictine in New York, just wonderful."

"Now that's strange," said I. "You accept my criticism of your poem but you uphold your country's bad liquor."

"Let me take you to a place where I can give you better Benedictine than you will find in France. Are you free to-night about 11:30? Very well. That's fine. Come to Tony's and you shall judge for yourself. You will? Well, be punctual. Last time I promised to meet a man there at eleven-thirty and he did not come till after midnight and I did not want to drink any more. But I saw on the list of drinks that Tony was serving absinthe frappé that night. It gave me a thrill. You cannot get absinthe even in France but we with Prohibition had it. I felt unreasonably proud of Uncle Sam. So I had an absinthe frappé and then I had another. Still my friend did not come; so I went on drinking. At last, looking to the doorway I saw him enter. I had had five absinthe frappés!

"I felt strange and uplifted. Mr. Graham, I felt like the Mother of God, I felt more cosmic than I have ever felt before."

Prohibition, it will be observed, has the power of heightening the effects of language even in a writer of bad ballads. The lady paused to give better emphasis to her striking phrase. I accepted her invitation and received some very indifferent Benedictine. I suggested that the name on the label be altered to "Bootleg Blessing" or "D. O. M.—*With the blessing* of *The Monks of Eighth Avenue.*"

CHAPTER X

Blossom-Land

"I DO not ask what the girls do during the day, as long as they arrive here each night fresh and fit. The manager of ——land loves each of his hostesses in turn, but I can't do that. It does not make for discipline. I want to keep this place under control and build it up. The girls are carefully chosen and they are an asset of the dance-hall. They bring custom. Men come here night after night to dance with the same girl. The hoofers also are useful to business. A man will come in with his wife; he does not want to dance with her nor she with him. He takes a hostess, she takes a hoofer. They have a happy evening; they don't get annoyed with one another. Or a plain elderly lady comes in without a partner; it is little pleasure to dance with her, she chooses a hoofer. It is not exactly jam for him, but he may get a big tip. Sometimes he makes a useful friend. A rich woman dancing-mad, unable to find a partner in her own set will find one here and adopt him, take him to her home, perhaps even take him round Europe with her. There are several known cases."

The Manager of Blossom Land mentioned the names of two well-known society ladies who had thus found male help.

"The girls also make useful connections. A Wall Street man used to come here regularly three or four nights a week and ask for Marguerite. He did not dance. He would sit with Marguerite in an arm-chair in a quiet corner upstairs and pretend that she was his pet daughter from ten till one. He simply wanted something to take his mind off stocks and bonds after the day's work. He paid for the full number of dances and from that the girl took 25% commission. And not infrequently she would find under her stocking a twenty-dollar bill. He petted her a little, but it was all very innocent. They talked of life. I don't think he ever made a date with her outside Blossom Land. If you look at the girls you will see they are superior. They all have self-respect. I could not vouch for their morals, but they still think a lot of themselves."

It was a magnificent dance-hall, with two platforms for bands and a cinema screen in between. It cost a dollar to enter. There was a cosy club-room where men could go and smoke if disappointed in love. There was a luxurious mezzanine floor where you could take your partner for intimate conversation. But it was not allowed to bring in liquor. The professional dancers were elegantly dressed—Lopez the Spanish girl with green robe and black kerchief about her head was an example in herself. But the dancers were chiefly of the clerk and shop-girl type. The men wore shabby ready-made clothes; the girls were showy. There were some very good-looking ladies and some wild ones. All the races in Europe seemed to be represented. It was a sort of League of Nations dance. There were few with whom one would have cared for conversation. Yet what education would have done for most of them! I suppose it is generally overlooked that in our life of to-day, there are so many de-educative activities that the ordinary education received at home and at school is more or less destroyed during adolescence; it is not sufficient bulwark against degrading influences. We used to think that education was wasted on girls. But it is clearly necessary now if only as a prophylactic. Civilisation eats away the dignity of womanhood; business deadens its intuitions.

Blossom Land dancing was a remarkable sight. They do not dance there as they do at night clubs or at fashionable hotels. It is more free, fanciful, picturesque. There is much more space and the dancers take advantage of it. The dancing is very ambitious. The ballet and the musical-comedy stage have infected the steps of the children of the dance-halls. In England popular dancing is much more disciplined and monotonous than in America. No Charlestoning or Blackbottoming is allowed at Blossom Land but there are some things done which would cause reproof in a London dance-hall.

The women are more unrestrained. They give their partners more joy. They lope along with long outstretched guiding arms and insurgent thighs; they do close-up minuet curtseys where the girl drips over the man's knee. They run and chew as they run, keeping tongue rhythm. Every now and then they kick up one leg behind as in a cinema kiss. One young fellow dances the whole time with his knee between the thighs of his beautiful partner. She is in a light frock of crimson silk under which is a short white petticoat, and then rather neat black bloomers. She straddles his leg sometimes in such a way that she seems to be riding a wooden horse; he holds her waist with an open hand; she languishes backwards and her loose hair trails toward the ground. She seems to be doing a tableau of woman's surrender. A more pretty type is the imitation Pavlova continually doing the dying swan, retiring one leg behind and scraping an arc on the ball-room floor in mock death.

A similar feat is that of hanging right down on men's lowered arms and pointing a toe straight to the roof. This seems to occur mainly in the Tango which is danced at Blossom Land with great variety. It is curious to see a boy pick up a girl with his two hands to her sides, her legs wavering artistically in mid-air. You do not need to be a spy to discover that all the girls wear bloomers. To my eyes as I sat at the side sipping my ginger-ale the festive coloured scene was an eerie piece of make-believe. It was difficult to see these gay partners as they were in their offices and shops by day, or in their homes. Two psycho-analytical views suggest themselves; one that their dancing was the language of suppression, the other that it was the expression of a neurosis caused by frustration in life in modern New York. But it is possible to give too much theoretic explanation to a simple phenomenon. Boys and girls are out for diversion. Restraint is off. They like dancing. Sex helps.

CHAPTER XI

Zelora's Ball

I BOUGHT Zelora for thirty-five cents but she cost me five dollars before the evening was through. "Which of you ladies would like to dance with me?" . . . Zelora was the first to smile, so I took her. She was tall and broad and deep and comely; she was sheathed perfectly in green silk; her pencilled eyebrows made black half-circles over her large baby eyes. Everything I did was cute. Between dances she took me by the hand and led me across the ball-room floor to the table where I sat. She was cute too. Everything was cute.

"Where do you come from? What part of the United States?"

"I come from way back."

"Not from New York?"

"Oh, I live on West End Avenue, but I was raised on a farm way back in Idaho. My father is a farmer."

"I guess you're a Mormon."

"Yes, I'm a Mormon."

"Right first time. You're the first Mormon I have danced with."

"Don't pull my dress up, honey. That's better."

"So you're a Mormon. Have you been sealed yet?"

"No, I haven't been sealed except at birth. I was never inside of a temple."

"Are you all alone in New York?"

"I live with my sister Zoar. She dances at Arcadia."

"She is a hostess there?"

"Yes, she's terribly good-looking, too."

"Idaho seems a very small state to me; looks as if one could jump across it."

"Guess it's a small state but the mountains are big."

"Did you ever do any farm work?"

With disgust . . . "No."

"But how did you get to be so tall and well developed?"

"Horseback-riding, climbing trees, climbing mountains, running."

"You look very well."

"Gee, I should say. I'm the smartest girl on this floor."

"Did you dance out there in Idaho?"

"Yes, most everybody dances there. There's nothing else to do. Gee, you should see the farm where I was raised. It's way down between two mountains. On one side you see Look-out Mountain. There's a beautiful waterfall comes down just by the gate."

In an interval of the dancing a girl came out and sang a popular song about the joy of getting a boy. I sat with Zelora at a table eating ice-cream. Those dancers who had not got tables sat on the floor of the dance-hall, and we watched a small revue. We heard a song about the Mississippi Delta:—

Muddy water in the street,
Muddy water on my feet,
But I love the Delta;
It's God's own shelter.

It was the time of the great spring flood of the Mississippi and seemed to be wrongly worded. But the song was a curious commentary on the theory that New York is not America. There I was at Roseland, the most popular dance-hall on Broadway. My chance partner was from Idaho and we were listening to a song about the Delta. New York after all does draw most of its colour and sentiment from the rest of America.

Zelora wanted to know where I lived and what I was doing and would I not take a ticket for a ball. This beguiled me to come again and spend a very gay and colourful night at this lively resort of the masses. I brought Helen and four or five others to the Arabian Night's Ball.

At eleven-thirty the following Tuesday night we passed through the din of the Turkish band at the door and were admitted into the midst of two thousand revellers. Mr. Burgess, the manager, who was extremely kind and hospitable, found a table for us and made me one of the judges of the costumes. Paul Whiteman was to come from his cabaret for a few minutes and give away the prizes.

There were sixty-five professional masqueraders taking part besides the hostesses and the hoofers and the general public.

There were sultans and jinns and caliphs and sorcerers and Aladdins and wicked uncles and Ali Babas, dreadful masks, alluring nakedness and somehow or other everything that was not Arabia as well—unless New York and the world itself is just an Arabian Night. And Zelora was my Scheherazade.

Noise, odour of naked bodies and crush. The police may insist on the discreet attire of the houris of the stage but they do not interfere with the revellers of Roseland. There were many young men made-up as girls exposing a large part of their bodies as if in defiance of the supposed fairer sex. What was chiefly against them was that they were mostly too tall. One of the most effective of them was introduced to me as Texas Guinan. She had Texas's blond wig and a mass of pearls and she imitated the tremendous voice of Texas. "May I leave this horror at your table for a little?" said Mr. Burgess.

This false Texas was nothing loath to partake of some gin—we had some with us and mixed it with ginger ale. She was a lively character and attracted a number of other dancers about us. Another male impersonator of woman came and showed us his step-ins which he alleged he had made himself; they were of pink diaphanous crêpe de chine and fastened with a tape. Over this fragile garment he had only a burnous but there was something incredibly ludicrous and bizarre in a man of six feet standing exposed for a moment in girl's underwear. He began to carry on a mock flirtation with Texas, encouraged by shouts of mirth from the others.

"Come together, girls," said the appalling blonde. "Let me tell you a story. Those who don't think they ought to listen, go away."

She turned to Claire, an artist of twenty-five or so, who looked very quiet and pure—"You, my dear, don't listen to this."

Claire looked annoyed.

"Well, there was once a widow who had lived too long in a state of moral restraint, and suffering from her ill-health she went to a doctor for advice. He said to Madam, 'There is nothing I can do for you. You had better marry again.'

" 'What sort of man do you advise, doctor?' asked the widow.

" 'Any young man with big boots,' said the doctor, "but stand back, you bourgeois, you won't get the point of this story."

The false Texas reeled off a series of stories which were more indelicate than amusing. I took Claire out to dance and left him. We agreed that there are limits to what one will listen to from a man dressed up as a woman. The dancing under the baton of Fletcher Henderson's orchestra was a riot. We were mixed up with moving tableaus. Intermingled with the normal masqueraders were groups who were also allowed to compete for the prizes. A man beating his wife accompanied by an imploring child were parading the ball-room. They were intended to represent the CURSE of PROHIBITION. In England they might well have been taken to be a living picture of the popular song—"Sell no more booze to my father." It's the cry of his heart-broken child. Another trio was a statuary group of the Village Blacksmith and his sons. They were frosted all over and looked as if they had fallen off a Christmas tree. A third group, evidently Russians, were labelled LOST IN THE STORM, a man, a woman, a little girl in torn clothes, their feet done up in sacking tied round with string. They trailed a baby sewn up in a quilt lying in a birch-bark sled. Their faces were pale and haggard and the realism of their make-up was so effective that Clare and I wanted to go to them and offer them money. They won the second prize for originality. That is a terrible category to be in, the second for originality, but there was a group which put all the others into the shade. It was called SHANGHAI SOLDIER and had the merit of being both topical and striking. A crouching soldier in soiled khaki was bearing on his back a raped and murdered girl. She hung there like a sack of flour. The soldier held a rifle with bayonet fixed covering a skulking Chinaman who was chained to his free hand. This apparition from China stalked the gay ball-room for half an hour and the soldier must almost have died from exhaustion.

Mr. Burgess asked me to be one of the judges and I gave my vote unhesitatingly for the soldier. I came to play quite a part in the ball. I sat in the middle of the floor and there were twenty-five parades of dancers past me. We had to choose for originality, charm and wit and there were first, second and third prizes in each category. Daddy Browning balancing a see-saw of peaches and sugar and leading on a string an unwilling goose easily won the first prize as funny man; the second was won by one of the men dressed as women. He called himself Black Bottom, was dressed entirely in black and owed his success to the serpentining of his body and his hips. A very funny Charlie Chaplin followed him.

Then we judges could not agree about a third prize for originality. I was in favour of a crippled newsboy, but there was clamorous demand for a one-legged soldier. I thought this soldier had really two legs but had hidden one of them in a remarkably clever way but I discovered that he was a war-victim and that the desire to give him a prize was purely sentimental. He and the crippled newsboy mounted the rostrum together and a vote was taken by acclamation. The soldier won.

A princess, a genie and a rose won the three prizes for charm. They also were judged by popular vote as there were so many beautifully dressed girls. I went about taking pretty girls by the hand and leading them to front so that they could be properly viewed. The Roseland hostesses were entered in a separate competition and a very chic bell-boy in trouserettes of light blue satin with little cap to match won the prize. I was sorry it could not go to my partner Zelora but Idaho did not know how to improve on her natural good looks and she was outmatched.

We were hours judging. It was three o'clock when Mr. Burgess waved to the band and said, "Come, let's dance again." Then the Shanghai soldier and Daddy Browning and the Orphans of the Storm and the wicked Sultan waving his scimitar and Scheherazade and the false Texas and the crippled newsboy and the forty thieves and the Honolulu girl and the beach-comber and the women in rompers and the geishas and the blind cobbler and the wonderful tailor and the statuary group and the Curse of Prohibition and the Civil War veteran still bearing the tattered flag of his regiment and the Egyptian figures wearing huge yellow and scarlet masks and the artists' models and the funny policeman and Helen and myself all danced.

Broadway outside rolled on the same as ever. What remained of our party went across the road to Roth's for roast beef sandwiches and coffee. While we sat there gaily discussing the ball the first workers of the morning began to come in for their breakfast coffee, their eggs and their wheat.

CHAPTER XII

A Rooming House in Speakeasy Street

IF I have not arrived at Easy Street at least I am on Speakeasy Street; I have a lodgment in the Roaring Forties. I live on the fourth floor, rear of a little old house which looks like a red flowerpot in a yard beside the lofty white business palaces which surround it. On the roof of a similar house which faces my window there are wind toys which revolve gaily, a juggler who throws mirrors, a gobbling duck, a black sheep who waggles his head, a windmill. The Street-door of the house is never closed; the tenants go in and out at all times of the night. They are actors, musicians, hoofers, bootleggers. Giant jars of alcohol, too big to steal, are delivered on the second floor—"Is there a speakeasy in this house?"—"I know damn well there is," says the always angry Mrs. Sullivan, who not only does the rooms in this house but in two others in the same street.

There is no elevator, the balustrade of the steep crazy stairs is broken as if some time or other drunken men had fallen through. The air is infallibly Irish but the place is hung with huge dusty German prints. No one knows exactly who is living in the house. There is one telephone; it is on the second floor and it rings all day. In the mornings no one answers it; all the inhabitants are asleep. Angry foreign voices try to tell us the names of the people they want to speak to. A notice in pencil says, "Will those who are not polite enough to take a message leave the telephone alone." Doors on various floors stand half-open all the evening and most of the night. You hear a medley of guitar-playing, songs, *bla-bla* of announcers on loud speakers, noisy discussions over cards. My nearest neighbour wears crimson and red pyjamas over his trousers and is forever on the stairs in this attire. The second-floor front is a large room where companions from Babel gather about a billiard table every evening. Second rear seems to deal in liquor. In the third-floor front two men in their B. V. D.'s dance to a gramophone. And ever and anon the telephone rings insistently, till some one is moved to lift the receiver and yell a name up and down the stairs.

My bootlegger, a young fellow with a Y. M. C. A. expression, comes upstairs laden with the stuff and calling my name. He sits on my bed and discourses on the merits of his rye which he sells only to be "cut." He brings me an unsolicited bottle of apricot brandy. "I can recommend it highly," says he. "It costs you only three-fifty the bottle." "Why, yes," I reply, "it would cost five dollars in London."

"And if you have any ladies visiting you," says he knowingly, "mix a little gin and apricot brandy; it has a good effect."

His car was waiting outside. He promises to come regularly.

When I took my room I was told, "This is a house where nobody interferes with anybody else's business." That has proved to be true. It is freer than a hotel. No one is looking for tips; there is no door-keeper. No one raises her eyes if you bring your dancing-partner from the night club to give her a drink at three in the morning.

One special sign of freedom is that no man ever smiles at you or gives you greeting. The women about the place may smile; the men never. The men have decided that they will remain strangers. That makes the place much freer. In the rooming-house on Speakeasy Street they do not speak.

CHAPTER XIII

"Burlesk"

A PERSON who makes disgusting noises in order to provoke mirth is a buffoon, so also is a fat man who deliberately amuses by his fatness. There is much buffoonery on the comic stage. It is a low popular taste. Burlesque stands theoretically higher. It is mockery through exaggeration. It is caricature dramatised. It is more witty and less extravagant than Extravaganza. But it may also be more brutal. Sheridan's play *The Critic* is a burlesque. *The Taming of the Shrew* is a burlesque. Somerset Maugham's *Our Betters* is a burlesque. But the word is seldom applied to true drama of that kind. The comprehensive word comedy has to suffice. The word burlesque seems to have been appropriated by a different type of entertainment. At least, in America. In Great Britain there are no burlesque shows. The expression would not be understood in London. In America "burlesque" is a revue where vulgar talk is mixed with naked girls. Its background is one of comic tramps, Jewish buffoons, and jocular policemen. Its object in entertainment is to provoke ribald laughter and cause physical excitement of a limited kind.

Probably it sprang into existence in the mining camp or as part of country fairs. There are many burlesque elements in the shows of a fair. Then it met the taste of the immigrant masses. It was first of all a men's show, and only later became one

"BURLESK"
"Just save a little ray of golden sunshine for a rainie daey!
It will come in mighty han'y when the skies are grey."

to which upon occasion respectable women could be taken. Even now the burlesque public is four-fifths men. Women are opposed to burlesque shows and if they had their way would close them all. And where churches abound burlesque tends to fade out. For it is an offence against decency. While I was in New York one was started near 3rd Avenue and 34th Street. It was not a success. Scouts were sent out with rolls of paper tickets to give away to men. Two passes were thrust into my hand: I went in. I felt I could not invite a lady to accompany me and in that I was right for it was exclusively a man's show and might reasonably have exhibited a notice—"Men Only." That is not to say that I did not have an amusing evening. Exuberant and Rabelaisian sex is less disgusting than a mean suggestive comedy of the fashionable type. But words were shouted by the audience that belong only to the barracks and the canteen and it is embarrassing to hear them in the company of women, though the girls on the stage invited them.

Some weeks later I passed the same theatre. It had become an ordinary cinema. I asked at the box office why the "Burlesque Show" had been abandoned. Had it been raided? I was answered laconically—"Too many churches in the neighbourhood. They killed it."

For Anglo-Saxons burlesque is a decaying taste. It does not seem to succeed in the American parts of New York, though it thrives on the East Side and in Harlem.

Houston Street Winter Garden is one of the most lively. Electric lamps display the word "BURLESK" at the foot of Second Avenue and in a glare of light, Jewish and Russian youth streams in to see the show. For this sort of theatre the premises are very elegant, "voluptuously appointed," is the expression. Some ambitious half educated European must be responsible. You climb no stairs; there is an elevator. At the entrance there is a notice—*Leave all your troubles behind all ye who enter here. Dante.* Some one must have said that the burlesque show was an inferno and so the proprietor translated afresh the words "Abandon hope all ye who enter here." Houston Street knows no better. A man who rhymes Dante with aunt. Above the proscenium the same hand had inscribed—*The Show's the Thing. Shakespeare.* Oh, Houston Street!

The chief feature of this show when I was there was undressing on the stage. The leader of the chorus, although but slightly robed, had five or six tiny garments which she could remove and still remain covered by police regulations. She and her troupe sang a popular song over and over again, dancing and posing and at each repetition she divested herself of part of her clothes, rapturously encouraged by the audience. The men knew by experience that she would never completely undress but cheated themselves into thinking that she might. Supposed not to like torment and illusion of this kind, they nevertheless applaud it. When the lady gets to a gossamer wrapping over a triangle of white linen the chorus whisks off-scenes and the curtain drips down before the eyes. "Boy, didn't that get you, how will ye sleep to-night after that?"

The theatre is filled with stout unexercised young men. They are male enough to produce a rather goaty atmosphere. They seem to swell before the entr'act and they wriggle in their tight ready-made clothes. There is something superheated about them and they communicate it to the stuffy air. But what a gross show! It is said that a girl has to weigh 150 lbs. to get a job in the chorus. The public eats the fat women with their eyes. They are crows and this is their carrion. The Celt and Anglo-Saxon like a glimpse of an æsthetic thigh; the Jew and the Slav like the full expanse of the broad bosom.

The big chorus came out and did ventral serpentines. The functionless and yet most lovely part of a woman's body fascinated like so many fixed spots. No wonder Solomon praised it in his beloved. But it seems terrible to expose it to unbelievers. It belongs to the artist, the lover and to God. And contortionism of any kind is loathsome. It is not only that but it is unpardonable that women should exploit their charms for the sake of brutal laughter.

The chorus with pink tassels attached to their nipples make their breasts revolve so they look like electric fans in motion. The "Kike" audience looks on with broad grins.

Half the programme was of this kind; the other

half contained more tolerable items of burlesque. These were vaudeville sketches, devoid of novelty and yet apparently always welcome. A man finding he has no money left and no shelter for the night decides that he will commit an offence against the law and so get a free bed in prison. "Now what shall I do?—I know, I'll pick a quarrel." He does so. A cop comes and parts him from the man he has begun to assault, addressing fatherly remarks to the one who was to blame and warning the innocent party very sternly. So that device will not do. "I know, I'll insult a lady." He does so. He insults her very ribaldly. The lady screams for protection. A cop hurries up and asks her how many times he is going to find her making a disturbance in that street, and he winks knowingly at the homeless man. That also has failed. He simulates being drunk. But this only produces affectionate concern on the part of the police, whose chief desire is for a share in the "stuff." In despair the homeless man rings a fire-bell. A woman rushes out and says, "You've saved my home. You splendid man! You hero!" and hands him a hundred dollars, and the woman leaves him standing bewildered with the notes fluttering in his hand. Then a policeman comes up and snatches the money from him, declaring it to be counterfeit. At this rough and tumble burlesque of police activity in New York the youths of the East Side laugh exuberantly. It is not so attractive as the girl show but it is taken as the bread of the sandwich after which there must be meat. Then sure enough out troop the girls again.

Another sketch as oft repeated, is of Bowery tramps, scratching out their fleas to an orchestral accompaniment, *crip, crap, bom.* A middle-aged dandy in evening dress appears to take pity on them, wishes to make them heirs to his millions. Various other street characters appear, among them a weatherbeaten drab. She reminds him of his mother. He becomes very sentimental and tells at great length of the change he is going to make in all their lives. They seem to believe him and are all ready to be taken in a limousine to his country house, when his keepers arrive and take him away to the asylum whence he has escaped—back to the "bug house." This also is in the true nature of burlesque and is diverting as certain European cartoons can be diverting, coarse, brutal and cynical in one and yet in a way a satiric comment on life.

Following the philanthropist comes the squalling chorus singing—

Save a little ray of golden sunshine for a rainie daey!
It will come in mighty han'y when the skies are grey.

Yes, the show's the thing, the girl's the thing. Hamlet should have provided a girl show for his wicked uncle and convicted him of sin that way. "Lecherous, treacherous villain!"

A poster on the bill-boards of the Chinese Theatre by Grand Street Station advertises—*"Fifteen Luscious Peaches on the Illuminated Runway of Joy"* joying at the Grand Street Burlesque. As the Chinese do not need to advertise their own programmes they sometimes sublet their bill-boards to others.

When the burlesque stage has a runway the girls have more sport with the audience. It allows them to be aggressive in their frolics. The men more or less passive in their seats flutter as the women "kid" them. "Oh, you old son of a gun, where's your wife?" . . . "Take 'em all off, go on!" . . . "Oh, say, look, he's bashful." The runway in short gives the audience as a whole a sexual organism. No wonder it gets excited as nakedness dances along.

The police raided the Fifteen Luscious Peaches and the show had to stop. The reporters at Police headquarters with whom I was at the time seemed all to rejoice as if their own opinions had just been voiced by public action. Whatever they were in their lives they were characteristically American in their views. According to them the police threatened next time to go on the stage and club the girls if they hadn't got more clothes on. A charming task for the police—another notch on the night-stick for every girl so clubbed!

What the police will allow or what not allow is however very vague in New York. It seems largely to depend on public opinion. The East Side wants burlesque. Harlem wants burlesque. "Hell's Kitchen" wants burlesque. But if these were ordinary American communities the burlesque shows would almost certainly be eliminated.

CHAPTER XIV

Libuse, the Crazy Waiter

LIBUSE is an artist in true burlesque. That is the name of the famous crazy waiter who scatters plates about your head, or for diversion gets under the table and bites the leg of your fair partner. His principal habitat is the Strand Roof, one of the most pleasant dining-dancings on Broadway, so pleasant that it has to be tempered by the presence of a mad waiter whose job is to annoy you facetiously. Directly I sat down a waiter hurried past me, brushing the top of my hair with the tray which he held in his hand. I frowned; but Patricia smiled. It was the crazy waiter, an odd man of medium stature, baby face and high obstinate brow, rushing about awkwardly and impetuously.

A spacious dancing floor faces a small theatre-stage, hung with brightly coloured curtains, and three ways round the floor and in three tiers go the white tables with their bottles, glasses, plates and gay company. Dinner costs between two and three dollars, but you must bring your own liquor and hide it. You dance between courses. There is a revue and you dance between the numbers of the programme. The most charming way to begin the evening is to go straight on to the floor and dance before taking a seat or ordering the dinner. People eat too seriously. The habit of application which belongs to the office-desk persists with many men and they are apt to gobble up their food as if at the restaurant also time were money. But the dining-dancing cures all that. You go slowly, you dance, you watch the revue, you get thumped on the back by the mad waiter.

Libuse is a Czech; there is a good deal that is Slavonic about him. He might well have played the part of *He who gets slapped*. His antics are not just horse play; he is not a Charlie Chaplin, though Charlie would play the part very well. I feel one could write much about Libuse. The running commentary of his burlesque dramatises the featureless story of eating. He is prologue, epilogue, chorus. He knows every fault of an offensive waiter, fusses round your table, breathes on you, brings you the thing you did not ask for, spills the soup, annoys your partner, licks his pencil point, and adds up long columns of figures in front of you. If a lady asks the way to the dressing-room he points it out most elaborately, taking her to the middle of the dance floor and indicating the way with gestures and saying, "The way to the telephone, Madam, is up the stairs at the back. You will see a little room on the right." Sometimes he pretends to escort new arrivals to a table and keeps bringing them to corners of the room where all the tables are already occupied, and then looks perfectly helpless.

At one point in the proceedings the head waiter pretends to intervene. "You cannot do this sort of thing," he says, "you are insulting the guests, I shall have to fire you."

"You cannot fire a union waiter," says Libuse, "no, sir. Do you say I'm fired?"

He takes out a whistle from his pocket and blows it shrilly. At that all the other waiters leave their posts and flock to him. A chair is placed in the middle of the floor and he stands on it and holds a mock-meeting of protest. He gabbles a long speech in imitation broken English and the only intelligible words seem to be the names of George Washington and Abraham Lincoln constantly repeated.

Threatened by a strike the head waiter is obliged to retain the services of the crazy waiter, and the fun goes on.

One of the revue company attempts to sing the sentimental song, "I'm all alone, I'm so all alone," and the waiter burlesques him by always being near him, in fact holding him most of the time, so that his song gets more and more absurd. Then he burlesques the leader of the orchestra; then he dresses up as a drum-major and fools about in front of a supposed military band swinging a huge baton. When dancing becomes general on the floor he appears with a large doll clothed in red and proceeds to dance with her in the most knowing way, doing the things which one ought not to do and yet does. Tired of that he handed his doll first to one man, then to another, and took their living partners instead. The male guests liked to show off with the red doll and the crazy waiter evidently enjoyed his dances with his chance-found ladies. As far as I could see he did not tread on their toes.

Somehow or other the harlequin remains the centre of interest the whole evening, his absurd childish face bobbing up here, there and everywhere. His pranks seemed infectious. The real waiters always seemed about to do something queer and the guests were on the alert not to be fooled. Frank Libuse must be very valuable to the proprietors of the restaurant. His doings are always discussed, and they are now becoming a regular topic of conversation with those who have been to the Strand Roof. I am told that Libuse is in considerable demand for private parties. A rich man asks a number of celebrities whom he does not know personally to come and have dinner with him and he engages Libuse to be extra man to wait at table. This should offer him more scope. I should like to see him spill grated cheese on the head of Mr. Bennett or let Mr. Wells sit in a chair that wasn't there, catch a fly on Margot, or offer to shave Mr. Shaw.

One of his favorite jokes is to come in with what appears to be a large stein of Münich beer, and forget who has ordered it. He wanders about the place in a dazed way while on all hands self-conscious drinkers shout to him, "Here, here!" This would be a wonderful stunt if the chief officer for enforcing Prohibition or the chief commissioner of police were present. But there is endless scope for a clever fellow like Libuse.

CHAPTER XV

Moskowitz

MOSKOWITZ'S pinky face is ruined by hot restaurant air, but it is benevolent with the reflection of the kitchen. Because of the Saturday night crowd it is at first difficult to distinguish him. He is not standing behind the elevated table on which his elaborate dulcimer is reposing, but wandering among the swarm of guests, exchanging local business news and Jewish witticisms. He does not feel urged to play to the sixty cent audience, those who are gulping down Rumanian food and hurrying to be in time at Gabel's Theatre or Houston Street Winter Garden. This first burst of customers is not preferred. When they are gone their places will be taken by those who think they get enough entertainment for the night at Little Rumania.

I find a place where there are already three young men, by their talk journalists, and soon gather that they work on the "Daily News" and are out getting copy. Not that they expect to find anything at Moskowitz's, but Little Rumania is their rendezvous. Their job is to find stories and I reckon they are at it most of the day and the best part of the night. I introduce myself without giving my name. I also am in the newspaper game. That is enough. We are all friends. Behind us are five garrulous Jewish girls, sallow, dark and ambitiously intellectual. In front of us stands the broad shelf with the dulcimer waiting like some half-played game of chess. Many men with dark close-cut knobby craniums are at other tables and with them fat expansive women. The tables are so close and so crowded that it is difficult to move among them, but a popular Jewish soloist manages to do it. He has no platform, but zigzags on the floor in the midst of the company, singing from his curious repertoire. There is a piano behind the dulcimer and there sits an old blind man and plays.

"He's no good now, can't play. But Moskowitz doesn't like to turn him away," explained one of the D. N. men. "It would break his heart if he had to stop playing."

Sometimes the old man gives way to a little girl who plays popular dance airs like "Baby Face" and "Ting a Ling." But she is not allowed to accompany the soloist. His name also is Moskowitz, but he is not related to the proprietor. He is a short slim fellow with a comic-looking bump which attracts the gaze to his head. Music sentimentalises him. His eyelids hang and his eyes look downward. It is as if matches broken in two kept his eyelids up, invisible matches. He wears a short-sleeved shirt whose cuffs are hidden, and his naked-looking hands drip down from the sleeves of his thin coat. His hips also seem to droop as if he were about to sit down—a musical mannerism or a sign of rhythmical bondage. He sidesteps jauntily among the tables, singing in a knowing way, but never addressing his song to any one in par-

AT MOSKOWITZ'S

Kosher broiled, *kitsi-kitsi-shitsi,* and the old man wants to play his dulcimer to the king.

ticular—not concert-room singing, not drawing-room singing, nor yet street singing—a sort of tavern mode of song—*Kitsi-Kitsi-Shitsi,* not deliberately Jewish, but sufficiently racial to be hypnotic to an imitator. A take-off of Moskowitz the singer would be a comic turn in itself.

At ten o'clock the scene in the restaurant is already fine. It is warm and glowing. Moskowitz senior mounts the rostrum and plays his famous dulcimer. He also seems to be greatly affected by his music. He and his dulcimer are almost legendary on the East Side. The common jibe is that he ought to be at the cash register and not mounted in front of an instrument, the proprietor, and a Jew at that. But he is a mellowed easy-going soul, not running Little Rumania to make a fortune, but because he loves it. He will never sell out and buy something bigger.

Moskowitz playing the dulcimer is a study for an artist. He plays it, head on side like a doctor listening intently to a pulse. His lazy curved nose sticks out as if scenting music. He is introspective. He rolls his tongue; his lips taste the meagre hairs of his moustache. Then suddenly the doctor pose has gone. He is more watchful, vigilant, stealthy. He raises one hand with its mallet, like a cat playing with a mouse or pawing at a dangling string. Rumanian music, Hungarian music, Russian music, French music—it is all at Moskowitz's command. Say what you would like him to play. He will be delighted to do so. Tchaikowsky's Ninth Symphony? Very well. Your favorite Brahms? Yes. Or merely Valencia? Valencia be it.

After eleven some of the richer East Side crowd come in for supper after the theatre; among them some very charming looking women in evening dress. Moskowitz plays the "Barcarolle" and one of them sings the words. The whole restaurant is hushed and the romantic glamour of Venice is realised. It is remarkable operatic singing and when the last strains die away every one applauds.

Moskowitz looks up whimsically from his instrument and nods down at our table.

"She steals my applause. I don't like it," says he facetiously.

A curious coincidence now occurred at my table. The man next to me began telling me about one of my own books.

I thought at first he was having a joke at my expense. "You know, I wrote it," said I.

"What?"

"I am the author."

"You are Stephen Graham?"

"Yes."

"I can't believe it."

"Nevertheless."

He proceeded to refer to various passages in the book and satisfied himself that I was not fooling him.

"Well, isn't that strange?"

The Jewish girls behind us had been listening.

He turned to one of them and she smiled. It made the party one with us. The girls turned upon me to devour me. I was amused that the fascination of the visiting British author held even in a foreign quarter of the city.

Moskowitz also heard. His ears were very quick. He came and shook hands and talked of his friend in the writing world, Konrad Bercovici, and presently brought an album in which were pasted various cuttings from the newspapers, referring to himself and Little Rumania. Like most other characters in New York he loved seeing himself in print. I was held to write about him and send whatever I wrote. "I fully intend to," I promised.

Little Rumania remains open most of the night on Saturdays, so I went out for a breath of the air of the Avenue and a change of scene. I went to Delancey Street and looked in at Philips' Russian Bavaria—this hybrid name is perhaps easily explained—Bavaria for beer and Russia for dance. Mr. Philips' invitation is, "Come to the Fountain of Joy." But it is not easy to get into this fashionable East Side resort unless you are known to the management. I showed my card and mentioned Haimowitz, another Rumanian Jew who has a lively dive in the neighbourhood, and I was allowed to stand in the doorway and look on. Mr. Philips hospitably offered me a cigar.

Russian Bavaria is a very ornate cabaret with restaurant tables and dancing floor, changing coloured lights and floral festoons. The crowd was the foreign élite, spending a good deal of money but showing much more. An examination in English might have yielded unflattering results, but they had the dollars and the appetites. While the East Side was well represented there were parties from several parts of New York and some from out of town who had come in big cars. There was a line of heavy automobiles outside. At half an hour after midnight there is not a vacant chair in the place, and customers were repeatedly turned away. One of the doormen kept coming down announcing newcomers, and Mr. Philips decided according to their wealth and desirability whether he would squeeze the others up and make room for them. Some he was loathe to turn away he asked to wait. The place reminded me of a Russian cabaret, in that the entertainers, hostesses, call them what you will, received very little open attention. They were enjoyed. But eating was the main obvious interest.

I looked in at Haimowitz's later and much the same thing was going on. Haimowitz himself was not there at the moment, and a waiter tried to understand me.

"Vot language do you shpeke?" he asked me at length.

"I do speak Russian but I usually am understood in English," I replied.

"I vill bring Russhen girl, she vill interpret for you," said the waiter.

Thanks to the Russian girl I received a club sandwich and an intolerably hot pepper. Haimowitz came up to me as I was going out and refused to let me pay my bill. "That's nothing," said he, "but I vill beg of you one favour, that if you write about me you vill not put my address." So I cannot say on what street this other epicure and entertainer regales the East Side.

For my part I preferred Little Rumania, found it more jolly and returned to listen to Moskowitz again.

At two in the morning Moskowitz's was as gay as ever. Male Jews were doing a step dance and their women partners were clapping in time. All the restaurant was watching. The D. N. men were still there. And when a child interrupted the dancing, got in among the men, one of the reporters exclaimed wrathfully, "That's what's the matter with this country—sentiment—it invades everything. So they let a kid spoil a dance. They are all petting that boy who ought not to be here at all."

The other D. N. man protested, "But think of more-ality," said he. "Where would the country be without more-ality? Mr. Graham, let us drink to more-ality."

"Yes," I said lifting my glass of near-beer, "More-ality, more and more of it."

Towards three on Sunday morning we strolled up Second Avenue, homeward, in still merry mood.

CHAPTER XVI

Round About Police Headquarters

THERE is a curious little street on the East Side called Centre Market. Some shops in it expose in their windows revolvers, night-sticks, policeman's boots. Doors stand open all night and alert-looking men dart in and out. There are lighted upper windows and back rooms. If you keep along a dark hallway you see a crowd of fellows in a poky apartment, smoking, conversing, sitting on tables, or banging typewriters, or talking into the grey mouths of well-used telephones. There is a string of cars in the roadway belonging to the police or detectives or journalists. On warm nights men are sitting on doorsteps or the sidewalk yarning. And their talk is constantly interrupted by the sound of fire bells. The men stop talking to count the numbers of the bells.

"No, listen, how many bells was that? The Bronx; not worth it. Let's wait for the second alarm."

If the bells are repeated it is the sign of a serious fire, and the journalists leap into their waiting cars and go to it.

There is a great building opposite, which looks like an old-fashioned railway hotel. It is Police Headquarters, spacious and solid, as if conceived by the heavy hand of the law, as if police boots had fired the imagination of the architect. It has an English note, strongly suggesting our Midlands, or Yorkshire. But it is an impressive building.

Here New York accident and crime are under one control. A long telephonic switchboard connects with every police station in New York and with much else besides, and men in shirt-sleeves and wearing ear-phones are kept continually busy all day, all night. That is high up in the building. On lower levels there are some curious rooms, for instance, a museum of finger-print records where the finger-prints of nearly every rogue in America are kept and also the prints of rogues in other lands. Here the itching palm has its code sign, and the desperado's fist its hieroglyphic. If our civilisation were lost and this museum discovered among the ruins, archæologists of another age would find something to test their powers of interpretation. Other rooms are devoted to those who watch bare legs in the interests of morality; others to the Pickpocket Squad, to the Bomb Squad, and so forth. For some reason not stated the Police think of themselves in squads.

I was introduced to a sombre-eyed inspector with tortoiseshell-rimmed spectacles, and he congratulated me on belonging to a country where there was still liberty, and I was amused to hear that from the Police.

Then I was shewn a large hall where each suspected criminal is brought and confronted by two hundred detectives with "camera eyes." This suggested a children's game to me. Despite the portentous gloom of the building I thought there was something exuberantly boyish about the Police. They enjoy the game of policing New York.

Outside, in Centre Market Yard, I met a Negro policeman just come down from Harlem in his spangling new Buick car to report on a case, one of about sixty coloured men in the New York force. He facetiously demonstrated to a knot of journalists how to embrace a woman in a two-seater car. Apparently he knew more about it than they did. After all, the Press is more serious than the Police. I became interested in his night-stick, which was all notched, as if he were a Robinson Crusoe and had been making a calendar on it. He explained that he put a notch on it for every man he had knocked out. On one side there were sixteen notches, these were ordinary knock-outs; on the other there were seven notches, they represented men with fire-arms.

One of the differences between New York and London is that our constables do not carry night-sticks. At sundown the New York policeman takes out this lively weapon, but it is only in riots in England that truncheons are used to persuade citizens. Still, New York offers much greater scope for head-cracking. Headquarters itself is at the centre of a mass of heterogeneous immigrants. It is hemmed in by swarms of Chinese, Italians, and mixed nationals from the old Russia. It is beleaguered by doping, bootlegging, and white-slaving. The very next street to it has been nicknamed Bootleggers' Row, and it is manned by a stalwart people who do not understand much English, but understand a night-stick more. One night a fire broke out there endangering a large supply of valuable liquor. The Italians successfully kept back both police and firemen while the "stuff" was being removed to another building. On the average it needs at least two policemen to persuade a belligerent Italian. When you see Italians defending a speakeasy you realise how Horatius kept the bridge in the brave days of old.

As I spent four nights a week all night round about Police Headquarters I obtained a vivid impression of the neighbourhood. The Italian quarter, often called "Little Italy," was the most remarkable. Upper Mott Street and Mulberry Bend must never be missed in a study of New York at night. There were religious festas in progress all the time I was studying the district, first one street in illumination, then another. In common with the business houses of New York that burn electric light all night whether in occupation or not, the Italians keep their coloured lamps gleaming till dawn. Often at five in the morning when all Italy had gone to rest I have gone down Mott Street and found it lit up from end to end with illuminated floral arches, crossing and re-crossing the littered street as if the Wise Men of the East were expected. In pride of place too, and unattended, stood a life-sized statue of the Madonna, waiting in celestial radiance for the world's homage. She wore a white robe with golden stars and a banner fluttering across the road explained her. It was the Festa Annuele Maria S. S. di Porto Salvo. It was two minutes' walk from Headquarters, and in company with police or press I often strolled round in the earlier hours of the night. At one in the morning it was a great sight. The street swarmed with Italians. On a crimson-covered estrada the height of the first floor of one of the tenements, a uniformed Italian band was playing clamorously led by a conductor in a grey Stetson hat. The Madonna at this hour was covered with dollar bills which had been pinned to her gorgeous robe by religious devotees. Arms and legs modelled in wax were also lying at her feet and wax babies with pins stuck into them holding dollars.

The street in its vivid reality would defy both painter and theatrical producer. Yet it had a marvellous theatrical quality. I would call the scene the "Transfiguration of a Slum." Drear red-brick tenements stare at one another in a narrow lane. But every window was open, and there were people with flashing eyes and florid faces at them. Each tenement window with its women and children looked like a box at a gaudy theatre. The iron fire-escapes were festooned with flags. There were trees of coloured lights on the sidewalks. The dense crowd flocking to and fro carried red and blue coloured balloons, some of which inevitably escaped and floated upward from the hot air to the moon.

MULBERRY BEND

A stone-throw from Police Headquarters Little Italy decks the night.

Meanwhile the band worked as if possessed, and the ear-dazed but happy crowds stared at the estrada with primitive joy.

I was much amused by a notice in an empty shop window, "WEVE MOVD ACROST THE STREET." That move must have been done at a quieter moment.

Perhaps the most charming piece of colour in the dazzling street festa was made by brilliant toy birds on strings, sold by men on the corners to the children. Birds for the children—and toy balloons and coloured snowflakes, confetti to cover the junk in the roadway, the old bedsteads, rusty stoves, broken-brimmed hats, bits of packing-cases, snail shells, mussel shells, broken fruit, and blustering old paper bags.

In all this wild scene the brave boys from Centre Market Street stand nursing their night-sticks in case of a row, and the florid Guineas eye them and register the American thought which is so briefly and yet adequately expressed by the word "cop."

This same Mott Street, however, not content with staging "Little Italy," becomes a little lower down the chief street in Chinatown, and very mysterious. It is hung with bulging paper lanterns. Its shop fronts are scrawled with Chinese characters. It has walls so heavily inscribed as to be called "Chinese Newspapers." It is densely populated by a mysterious secretive people, made to seem more mysterious through the flamboyancy of their Italian neighbours. When the journalists get tired of waiting for news they take a walk down the haunted thoroughfares of Oriental New York, and often pick up a more lively paragraph of news than if they had waited in their booths in Centre Market Street. For not all the news of a great city filters through from the police. Chinatown is packed with good copy though it is just a little dangerous to go and get it.

I suppose however the routine of the leg-men, the night reporters, tends to be tedious. There are hours most nights of the week when New York seems to sleep like a babe. The switchboard at Headquarters is quiet. There are no murders, assaults, burglaries, accidents. Even the fire-bell is silent. Nothing is signalled from any of the stations. The millions are carrying on quietly without need of first aid of any kind. The police and press are seated peacefully, doing cross-word puzzles or yarning about horses and bets or talking in habitual strain about the evils of Prohibition.

And yet there is a haunting feeling that you never know what the next moment will bring forth. I imagine some curious spirits in heaven hover near the Recording Angel a good deal of the time. And perhaps there are hours in eternity when little is stirring down below, and the world is good, comparatively good—the Recording Angel probably does not record small type happenings. But there is suspense round about him when his quill is quiet. The curious spirits, if not purged of morbid interests, are hoping for a crime.

"I'm just longing for a bit of news with a kick to it," says a young "Times" reporter. "Nothing has stirred me since the nigger killed the detective last week. Let's go to the Bowery for a roast-beef sandwich!"

"Let's go in," says a stout fellow on the "News," "Let's go in and wait to hear of twelve dead Chinks found on a cellar floor, all decapitated."

"Oh, boy!" says the Count to me one night. "You missed a murder, happened at 11.15, a pippin."

The Count was a very smart fellow on the "Telegraph." He was especially thoughtful for me and more hospitable with news than journalists are wont to be. He took me round and did me the honours of Headquarters.

On the night of the Dempsey-Tunney match there was a packed crowd of detectives, police, old inspectors, and what-not, in the "Times" room, for it was provided with wireless, and the fight as it came over from the loud-speaker was followed with intense interest. One of the chief matters discussed was whether the fight was a straight one; the police contending that it was straight and clean, the journalists being very cynical. But after the fight a very quiet night ensued. The New York crowds were behaving themselves. Somnolence settled down on Centre Market Street. I came in about two in the morning. One reporter was asleep with a newspaper over his face; another was reading a volume of Conrad. Two others were doing puzzles.

"It's been awfully dead around here for some time. No action. I catch myself longing for a big fire," said one.

"Anything to-night?"

"No. Nothing. A rumour of a suicide at the Waldorf."

"Police reported it?"

"No, nothing official. The cops are holding it, sure. Nothing ever gets out of the Waldorf."

"Say, the Waldorf can't hold back a thing like that. It's bound to get out in a few hours, anyway."

The sound of some one snoring came from a neighbouring room. The man with the newspaper over his face did not stir.

Half an hour later an old Irishman came in, grizzled, lean, smart, loquacious. Extraordinary to see a man of sixty do this young fellow's job of leg-man! But he was very spry.

"Say, the 'City News' has got something on that suicide," he informs, standing in the doorway. "It seems like this—the B. family habitually stay at the Waldorf from middle September to end October. Mr. B. went to Philadelphia to see the fight and he was a wild Dempsey fan. Yeh, he was all in on Dempsey. He got back to the hotel about ten o'clock, and after thinking things over decided to put himself out of commission."

"Good enough."

The man with the paper over his face wakened up, threw the paper down, yawned, and exclaimed:

"Yeh, that's the story."

"Say, boys. This is how I figure it. We ring up the Waldorf now, tell them the story, and ask if there is anything they would like to add, anything they'd like to straighten out for the sake of the family."

"Yeh, or ask one of the boys on the 35th Street Station to run off with the story to the Waldorf."

"Have the 'Times' a man there?"

"Yeh."

So the whole story appeared in the Press next day, wrested from discreet silence. Even a newsless night may be made to yield news through the desperation of ennui sometimes.

One night we were sitting on the doorsteps talking when a hatless man with pomaded yellow hair, spotted bow-tie, and gesturing hands, came hurrying out of Police Headquarters.

"You all reporters?" he asked. "Boys, come together! I want you to do something for me. You all have mothers. I want you to do this for me, for an old mother's sake—kill a story."

We closed about him sentimentally. "Wait a minute," said the Count, "before you tell us what it is. Remember, we haven't the power to kill a story. You should go to our bosses for that."

"It's like this. Half an hour ago my brother committed suicide. You all know him. Some of you have had pleasure from him. He is a well known vaudeville actor, but he has had a run of bad luck lasting months. To-morrow is his little girl's birthday and he had nothing to give her and could not give her a party. He's always given her a party till this year. I think it must have preyed on his mind, though I never guessed how he was feeling. I want you to make it accidental death. Not for my sake, but because of his old mother in Chicago. I feel that if she saw it in the papers that he had killed himself it would be a terrible blow to her."

This was of course very futile. I saw two reporters slip quietly away, get into a Ford, and go off.

"It's bound to get out," said the Count. "You can't kill it. How old was he?"

"Only thirty-three. It's my younger brother. I was with him till two o'clock this morning; he seemed quite cheerful."

"Not been drinking?"

"No."

"How did he do it?"

"Hanged himself on the end of the bedpost. I came in about three and found him like that. I cut him down, laid him on the bed, and telephoned hospital. But he was dead. I said to myself, 'I must keep this out of the papers somehow,' and rushed to P. H. Q. I've been in there talking it over, and they agreed to keep back the news while I went out and tried to get you on my side."

"No, you're wrong there," said one of the reporters. "The police slip with the news was handed out same moment as you came out. I've read it. The A. P. has it by now. Not that we don't sympathise and all that."

"Yes, we'll do the most we can," said the Count. "But we couldn't kill news if we tried. If you take my advice you'll cable a friend of your mother at Chicago to keep the newspapers away from her this morning."

"Try and make it appear an accident," repeated the brother helplessly. "We'll do the best we can," chorused the reporters. And the actor, for no doubt he was an actor too, put on his hat which he had been waving while he talked, and left us.

The knot of reporters broke up. "Well," said one, "I guess we've got the story anyway. No need to go up there. Fred and Ike slipped off. I wondered what they were up to. Of course they went straight to his lodgings. Still, I think we've got all we want, haven't we? Every paper's bound to run the story to-morrow."

A fire-bell sounded and all listened and counted the rings. "Rivington Street," remarked the fat man on the "News." "I wonder if it's a real fire. One of us might go over. Have you your police-card?"

The actor and his little child and the Chicago mother seemed quickly forgotten. A window had opened in New York and we had peeped in on a tragedy. Then suddenly the window was closed and the quiet night went on.

The Rivington Street fire proved smoke without flame. We returned to the Centre. A drunken pressman who had stayed too long in a speakeasy was there then and was trying to explain the Fourth Dimension to the others—

"That's something I *can* tell you about. Now, a Harvard professor has lately proved its existence. Look here. First there is length, then breadth, then width, and then, oh boys, then there's something more. You've got to get away from that . . ."

"But why?"

"You've got to because . . . oh, it's the realm of the spirit. You've got to get away from the material estate."

"Real estate for me."

"From materialism."

"Oh, ism. What do you mean, go into a convent?"

"A convent, a convent. Yes, I've got you. A convent."

"Come on, tell us what that Harvard bootlegger said."

"Talk like that, I'll beat you up!"

"You would?"

"I'll knock Hell out of you!"

"I'd lay you out with one hand tied behind."

"Is that so?"

"Is that so?"

"Broadway! On, boys! There's been a raid on a night club. Upper Broadway."

"Yeh—that's our dimension, I guess. Come on!"

A raid on a night club in London always means a police raid. The police come to arrest those selling liquor after hours and to take the names and addresses of those drinking it. But in New York it is much more commonly a raid by bandits. Such was this one. A couple of gunmen had entered a dance club, robbed the guests in Dick Turpin style, and got off in a high-powered car. A frequent occurrence—part of the "kick" in night club entertainment.

When we got to the club we found two couples still dancing indolently as if nothing had happened. "When we have big takings we usually send it to the bank under armed escort. But to-night there was not so much," said the proprietor. Some of the robbed guests had remained and were receiving their entertainment on credit.

It partly explained a joke I heard Barney Gallant make one night.

"I want some one to volunteer to be murdered here," said he. "I want to raise my cover-charges. But we have not had a raid or a murder for some time, and it's not good publicity. Any lady or gent ready to be murdered for my sake, please step forward."

But I found both the journalists and the general public more cynical about the staging of crime than the police, whose rôle evidently always was innocence. The plain-clothes men tell a great many stories, but they are mostly about genuine crime. At the same time they seemed to be on quite friendly terms with the crooks. I stood with one in the arcade at Times Square and was greatly amused by the nods, winks, greetings, he received from the sharpers he was there to watch.

My nights were packed with adventures of one kind or another, often charming, only sometimes eerie or horrifying. I had a childish desire to see a New York fire and nursed the card which was to permit me to pass the fire lines. But until the burning of the Sherry-Netherland tower I did not see the sort of fire which gets the front page. However, one night I saw two small fires, one of them nearer than I bargained for.

I was lying in my pyjamas waiting for the night to get older—I generally did not leave home before midnight—when I was wakened by the bell of a fire-engine. I raised my window indolently and looked out, and what was my surprise to get my hair and eyebrows singed by an uprush of flames and sparks. The fire was below me, in the same house, on the fifth floor. I jumped into my best suit, slung my diary, manuscripts, razors, suspenders, into a bag, looking feverishly round to see what I wanted to save, snatched up a packet of letters and a portrait, grabbed some more clothes, and made my exit. I altruistically knocked up the lady living in the next room to mine. She stood there ashen white and speechless, making the sign of the Cross. Meanwhile outside pandemonium seemed to reign, the yelling of fire-bells, rushing of fire-escapes, shouts, surging arrivals of new fire-engines, and the increasing murmur of swarms of people collecting and looking on. Without collar or tie or socks, carrying my bag, I was like a character escaping in some picture of a sensational film. We flocked down the stairs, excited and timorous. But the fire was extinguished in five minutes. In ten minutes the engines had all gone away and the murmuring crowd had disappeared.

I returned and dressed properly, took the El. and went to Centre Market Street where the boys were much amused in hearing of the adventure. Two hours later, in answer to a fire-bell, we ran round to the Bowery and saw a much more spectacular fire. A tenement house was ablaze. Like dry wood and petrol the rotten structure leapt into great conflagration, dimming the moon. The extremely smart fire brigade was already in charge, but I shall never forget the swarms of men and women in their underclothes or nightdresses packing the windows and swarming down the fire ladders, looking like hundreds of shrouded dead unnaturally revealed in the tremendous brilliance of the fire. But the firemen here, as everywhere in New York, had enormous supplies of water at their disposal, and suddenly the mass of flames changed into a great white cloud of hissing vapour in which we were all hidden, and flame never got loose again. In ten minutes all was over. No one was burned. It was not even small-type news.

"Fire any good?" queried a reporter when we got back.

"No, only a smear," said the man with me.

All the same I felt something of the primitive appeal of fire in my blood. Nothing else happened that night. When I got back to my lodgings I found the street-door had been locked. I had to go in next door, operate the elevator myself, and get up to the roof, the only way into the house where I lived at that time being through a trap-door from above. There I found an old rocking-chair, and I sat in it a long while looking over the wide circle of the still flashing and jewelled city. I could not see the pavements down below, but I had found a place of coolness and peace, aloof from the hard reality of the city. Only its beauty and mystery spoke to me, that and the serene sky above, which with its infinite stars seemed like the switchboard of the universe. I suppose when our old world goes up in flame, bells will sound somewhere. Exciting? Perhaps a small-type affair.

CHAPTER XVII

Chinese Theatre

THE Chinese in their limited way are more dignified than other New Yorkers. They do not go to burlesque theatres. They might provide that sort of entertainment for others, but not for themselves. The Chinese male is not excited by undress. Or if he be naturally excited by it, still it is not enough to pay for. Perhaps he does not prize getting excited and will not even pay to have his emotions aroused. Yet he is evidently devoted to his own theatre.

Wherever the Chinese are in considerable numbers they have their theatres. Thus in San Francisco you may see the same theatrical performances as in New York. But in London you will not see any, which is a fitting commentary on our supposed Chinatown. We have no great extent of Chinese population—Limehouse is exaggerated for literary reasons. New York has a large and growing Chinese population. The children checked in the cloak-rooms or waiting in rows in the vestibules of the Chinese theatres remind one that it is not enough to exclude Chinese by immigration laws. There are sufficient China-women to carry on the race in New York.

All New York gleams at night with chop suey restaurants. Formerly one had to go to Chatham Square for a Chinese meal, but now in Greenwich Village, or Yorkville, or upper Broadway, or Harlem, wherever you climb up from a subway station the coloured lights of the illuminated letters CHOP SUEY greet you. Some Chinese must be amassing wealth as restaurant proprietors. But the rich Chinese are very unostentatious. They do not emulate the Whites, do not come out in frock coats, do not remove to Park Avenue, do not roll forth in bright Cadillacs, do not cohabit with expensive mistresses. Instead they amass real wealth, buy jewels and eat vast quantities of their own terrible food. They go to their own resorts where the Whites are exploited and spend twice as much as the Whites. It is curious to see a party of Chinese merchants at Delmonico's, in that exaggerated Chinese atmosphere produced for tourists, perfectly at home, shovelling down chew mein as if their mouths were gates to all Asia.

China at least does not imitate America. Her theatres are trap-doors leading back to China. One of them is the old German opera house, the other some nondescript East Side theatre once used for vaudeville or Yiddish shows. I did not enquire how long they had been in Chinese possession. But they were probably in need of repair when they were handed over. The Chinese are indifferent to gilding and plush and stucco statuary. Exteriorly they are as drab, these theatres, as doss-houses. No paint: no flaring posters: no signs. You might pass several times before noticing that they were theatres. Interiorly they are so ramshackle that you could imagine rats running about among the legs of the indifferent audience.

There are women as well as men; they are all Chinese and all eating seeds. What is being performed is not drama in the Western sense. It is some sort of non-religious ritual in which great use is made of symbols. There is no realism. It is bizarrely fantastic. The actor lies down a few moments when he is murdered; another waves a flower and he is in love. There are no curtains, no exits. The scene-shifters work in full view of the audience, slowly changing a gilded throne to a four cornered canopy over a bed, or whatever it may be, one scene melting into another without interval or entr'act. Tablets of Chinese script hang from the roof and these roll up or are changed or moved, like religious banners in church.

The orchestra is a one-stringed fiddle, a man who beats with sticks on a wooden drum, cymbals and squeakers. It makes a queer row, but it is articulate; it follows and interprets or at least sympathetically accompanies the action on the stage, behaving like a choir of knowing birds. The performance goes on for four or five hours to be discontinued in the small hours of the morning and resumed next night.

The actresses in brocade kimonos with tinsel birds and flowers wear ribboned head-dresses and engage in long dialogues in bird-voices. A man with long black hair and a gold spearhead fixed to the centre of his brow takes advice apparently from his antique prospective father-in-law. They bow to one another countlessly. The girls retire behind curtains and sleep. The competing rival lover in silver mail affronts the gentleman with the gold spearhead. A large bespangled mother interrupts their quarrel. But the account of it is more intelligible than the presentation itself. It is not like a foreign cinema where despite ignorance of the language of the captions you can pick up the threads of a story. Action is interminably delayed. The sleeping girls come out of hiding and talk against one another like canaries once more, and only the spasmodic orchestral raptures, squeaking, rattling, permit you to believe that something really is happening.

Hours of it! And, oh, the fleas that mount along one's trouser-legs! These are Confucian fleas making West East in one love-feast. No Chinese objects. No Chinese pays any attention to me or to the fleas. We don't exist for him. Occasionally there is laughter at some hidden joke. But for the most part the Chinese are like students obsessed by the words of a professor.

Outside the theatre, the gloomy Bowery, roofed by its iron railroad and floored by cheap shops, bars, flop-houses, drunken men and with its lazy trolley-cars crawling by is non-existent. It is a mere shadow, something in a different plane. The trap-door of the theatre at least effectually disenchants the reality of the Bowery. Is the Bowery real? No, it is just something which China never imagined, something that no wise old man thousands of years ago ever saw in a dream. The only visions of the future which Chinese have must be Chinese futures.

CHAPTER XVIII

The Bowery

THE Bowery is one of the most remarkable streets in the world, combining features of the Cowgate in Edinburgh, of Limehouse Causeway in London, and the Khitrof Reenok in Moscow. In America it is unique. Other cities have their petty Broadways and ambitious Avenues but none has a Bowery. The denizens of other cities will say that the Bowery is not worth repeating, but it would be truer to say that it cannot be repeated. The Bowery has not been made; it grew, and even if it be a fungoid, it is natural.

Here is the street which *par excellence* stands outside the law, the great city's street of adventure, its Alsatia. Apparently, it has always been a dark mysterious place. Where now is the shadow of the black Elevated Railway was once the gloom of a dense forest into which the first Dutch settlers let loose their superannuated negro slaves, and savages met savages there—as they do to-day. The Bouwerie became Bowery Lane and then plainly "The Bowery." In a volume dated 1868 and entitled *Secrets of the Great City,* I read:

> The Sunday law which seems to be so rigidly enforced in other parts of the city is a dead letter in the Bowery. Here on Sunday one may see shops of all kinds—the vilest especially—open for trade. Cheap clothing stores, concert saloons, and the most infamous dens of vice are in full blast. The street, and the cars traversing it, are thronged with the lower classes in search of what they call enjoyment. (*Always that horrible*

habit of the lower classes.) At night all places of amusement are open and crowded to excess. Roughs, thieves, fallen women, and even little children throng them. Indeed, it is sad to see how many little children are to be found in these vile places. The price of admission is low and, strange as it may sound, almost any beggar can raise it.

A remarkable feature of the Bowery, this power of the penniless. Even to-day the beggars of the Bowery all seem to be able to get enough drink to be dead drunk by midnight.

The writer of 1868 goes on to tell of the immense German beer-gardens "handsomely frescoed and otherwise adorned," no doubt in the neighbourhood of that massive, decaying, never repaired German Opera House which now serves the Chinese as their most substantial theatre, where every night occult Chinese drama is spoken across the stage to a thousand Bowery Confucians and to the pallid faces of Beethoven, Liszt, Mozart, upon the walls. But where are the five thousand Germans who used to sit in the Atlantic Garden and swill beer on the Sabbath in defiance of the law!

Respectable people avoid the Bowery, as far as possible, at night; but on Sunday night few but those absolutely compelled to visit it, are to be seen within its limits. Every species of vice and crime is abroad at this time, watching for its victims. Those who do not wish to fall into trouble should keep out of the way.

Thus, 1868.

In 1927 it is still the most curious and most adventurous street in town, and it is the place in New

York where the Prohibition Law and other laws are most openly set at nought. The condition of its inhabitants between midnight and dawn is a dreadful commentary upon bootlegging. It is commonly said that Prohibition lets the rich man have all he wants but denies alcohol to the poor. But this is an illusion: the poor are more drunk than the rich, and for truth of comparison one should not in future say, "drunk as a lord," but "drunk as a beggar on the Bowery." In the Bowery the liquor is cheaper and stronger than in London, cheaper and stronger than it was in the Bowery before Prohibition.

There is something curious about the free surge of alcohol on the East Side. I go into a saloon there and I ask for a drink and I get it. How is it that in other parts of New York I have to take such precautions and go through a sort of ritual? I go to places where the doors and walls are perforated, and uneasy eyeballs flicker through the wood, peering at my face and form. I have to place an extended palm on a glass door or give a certain sort of tattoo with my knuckles. At that resort where I met Laura, when asked who I am, I must answer that I am Mrs. Worsfold, whoever she may be. I say I am Mrs. Worsfold and straightway I am admitted. I cannot get in as Stephen Graham. At some places I present a mysteriously scrawled card. At others I have to be known by my face. But in the Bowery at any of a score of saloons I just go in and get served.

Reeling helplessly, drunks come out at the little swinging doors and collide with indifferent policemen and fall helpless on the pavement, as if they were articles of human garbage discharged from some window by an East Side family. One night I saw four staggering drunkards holding on to one another while they sang and tried to play "Ring-a-Roses" round an indulgent cop, who handled his night-stick knowingly and yet refrained from cracking any skulls. Drunkenness seemed to be not even a social offence.

Sometimes I wonder if the pass-word and peep-hole business is not merely part of the glamour of the speakeasy, possessing considerable commercial value. The sophisticated like the thrill of imagining they are entering a smuggler's cave—an extra kick is imparted to the bootleg Scotch. Perhaps after Prohibition is withdrawn the romantic customs of this time will be retained, and you will still have to give a secret sign before entering a respectable bar. But is it not true that all the secret drinking places in New York might to-morrow begin to do open business without more interference on the part of the law than they suffer to-day?

"I don't think it makes much difference," said one saloon-keeper to me. "If it has been decided to raid the place the place will be raided. The police and the revenue officers have every bar in New York listed. The business we do is known. If you want to find a place to get a drink, ask a cop."

Another said to me, "The first day we opened up the police came right in, four of them, to be stood drinks, and I've had these four cops on my side in this business from that day on."

Not far along a side-street was another saloon, gloomy, dusty, and padlocked, with a printed notice, "Closed for the infringement of the Volstead Act." The saloon-keeper there had got on the wrong side of the authorities, I suppose, and his establishment was closed and placarded as an advertisement of Enforcement.

When I was last in New York, three or four years ago, there was very much less open drinking. The old bar-room was still under a cloud. Many were being converted into pool parlours, soda fountains, lunch counters, and cigar stores. A drunken man on the street gave one pause. Drink was more precious, drinking more sacramental. It seemed to me that the non-observance of the law was too trifling to be a serious reflection on the serviceableness and validity of Prohibition, and I said so. Although I have real pleasure in wine with my meals, and think a good dinner without some Burgundy or champagne a crippled feast, I have never denied the advantages of enforced sobriety. I hate the cheap saloon here as elsewhere and would gladly close or civilise a hundred of the worst public houses in London. The alliance of bestial drunkenness and prostitution is appalling. But there is some latitude between plaster-saint and drunkard—some space for civilisation. There is a great deal in the Bowery which may justifiably enrage the convinced "dry," and there are some things to enrage the convinced "wet," and there is the extenuating circumstance on which both "wet" and "dry" might be pleasantly at one.

When I first visited the city fourteen years ago I walked the streets of the East Side very much as now. There were many fewer drunken men about then. But there was an evil prevalent which seems to have disappeared. At that time certain saloons swarmed with unfortunate girls. The neat-waisted hackneys of the Bowery went in and out of the saloons like wasps. It was a distinctive sight of New York. The plain-clothes men who grafted on them brought a few of them to the Night Court just to keep up appearances, but they swarmed beyond the limits of courts and ordinances.

It is a remarkable fact that the saloons operating to-day do so without women. It is an unusual thing to see a woman of any age, young or old, in a Bowery saloon, and the numbers that lie huddled in corners at night is in the ratio of one to fifty, I should think. Prohibition may not have prohibited drink, but it has to a great extent prohibited public immorality. I believe also it has very greatly reduced drinking by poor women. A woman waving her arms and screaming, a street-corner fight between inebriated women, a staggering drunken girl being pushed into a taxicab—common sights in Whitechapel—are rarities in the Bowery.

Studying New York at night, I spent many more

hours on the Bowery than on Broadway. I felt there was a good deal more going on there than met the eye at first glance. A stone's throw away from the centre of it is Police Headquarters. "Bootleggers' Row" lies between, operated and protected by stalwart Italians. The west side of the Bowery is comparatively free from liquor, but the east side of the street is dotted with saloons, and possesses sometimes two to a block. They sell what is locally called "Block-fall"—you take a drink of it and are guaranteed to fall on the sidewalk before you walk a block.

Until the theatres discharge their audiences the roadway is considerably cluttered up with cheap cars. Dancers and diners in Chinatown, or at the alley-way resorts, leave their cars in the Bowery. It is not a place of motor thieves. Roofed by the ironwork of the Elevated railway, it is always eerie, and those who walk along the pavement awaken the curiosity. About midnight the Yiddish theatre empties, and somewhat after one in the morning the two Chinese theatres. I am most familiar with it at two in the morning. It is a strange restless street even then. Tramps lurch through it, unshaven, tatterdemalion, vociferous, predatory. For some reason they are often called "longshoremen" but it is a misnomer. They are plain ordinary hoboes. They bum food from restaurant to restaurant; they surround any isolated respectable traveller and beg smokes and the price of a meal in such a menacing way that it almost amounts to a hold-up, and he is glad to hand out dimes and offer the cigarettes just to get away unscathed.

The doors of a score of little hotels stand open with little lighted mouths which make them look like mousetraps set in a basement kitchen, waiting for mice when the world is asleep. For thirty-five or forty cents you may doss for the night, get a "flop in the Bowery." What suggestive names they have: "Niagara," "Defender." To apply the phrases "cheap joint" or "fifth rate" to these is quite wrong. They are special unclassifiable places. If the Bowery is a sort of republic, they are its Carlton, its Ritz. I was much tickled to see one called "The Savoy." After staying at the Savoy in London one might come to New York and say with quite an air, "I am staying at the Savoy for a while." Yes, at the Savoy in the Bowery. Where the original Indians and their successors, the Dutch slaves, lay under the trees and listened to the tree-toads, there are now strange caravanserais where strange men toss in old beds and hear the roar of elevated trains.

Yes, these places are first class. There is a ladder of night of which they are the top rungs. You must go down to Battery Park to see the bottom rungs, where, spread on dirty copies of the "World," hopeless and helpless derelicts lie face-downward on the frosty grass. Those who sit the night through on the divided benches of the asphalt park at the exit of Delancey Street are a rung higher, higher by some tiny line of hope;

huddled, they pass their cold hands to their grimy, hairy chests, cower in their rags, and wait for morning.

Oh, they are aristocrats who dwell in the Salvation Army rooming house. In London to sleep at a Salvation Army doss house means to be very low down. It is rougher faring than at a municipal lodging house or Rowton House. And, poor as London is, we have nothing quite so grim as a real East Side "flop house." I imagine it is called a "flop" because you just go in and flop down anywhere. But to "doss" does imply lying down and, most probably, implies taking off one's clothes. Derelicts in London are seldom so helplessly drunk as those in the Bowery of New York. They may take on more liquor, but they carry it better, or rather it carries them better—it is not so poisonous, not so dazing. Under the appalling influence of "moonshine" the East Side hobo merely wants a quiet place where he can fall down and remain undisturbed.

There used to be a place at Walworth in South-east London where parallel bars were provided, and the homeless, with their arms over these, hung like old clothes on scarecrows in a field. A dark room full of these hanging men was an appalling sight, but it is a thing of the past. The scene approaching it most nearly is that of the Bowery Mission Room at two in the morning.

There is a gloomy wire-protected window with an electric cross for a shop sign. A wooden door opens into a long room. It is one of the few places of such shape and appearance which prove not to be Bowery saloons. I have visited it at various hours of the night. But the first time it was considerably after midnight. I went in, went right through, visited the apartments at the back, and came out again without any one addressing me a syllable. The sight was extraordinary—some two hundred or more ragged men sitting on chairs in the dark, sprawling forward over the backs of chairs, or resting their heads on their wrists as if in prayer. Ahead of them on the far wall was a black cross, somewhat blacker than the shadow in which they rested, and the men looked as if plunged in dreadful penitence and dejection, hideously unforgiven. There was some lettering beside the cross, visible, I suppose, by day. I examined the words and found they were *Jesus Sees.*

I then found the night orderly of the establishment. He was on the Bowery sidewalk, smoking a cigar and chatting with the tramps as they passed. The doorway at that hour proved to be the rendezvous of all the alcoholised derelicts of the Bowery. Some had been lying for hours on bar-room floors and been kicked out, some had been lying in doorways and had sobered a little owing to the cold. They walked uncertainly like somnambulists, their eyes not dilated by intoxication but narrowed or filmed by narcotics. Their boots were burst and tied on by one or two holes with string; many were without shirts and had foul coats buttoned or safety-pinned or string-tied close to their Adam's apples. Their rags might easily have been bettered from what is thrown out of the windows of Mott Street or Mulberry. Apparently they were too "down and out" to seek that so easily obtained better clothing. It was as if the uncollected garbage of the streets had become animated and legged. Deucalion threw stones behind him and they became men, and civilisation has thrown balls of filth in the Bowery and they have become human, though by their looks they would hardly be able to repopulate the earth.

A genuine drunk may be a funny person. One listens indulgently to a vociferous gesticulating Froggie who has lost his way and his balance in the back streets of Paris. And a Cockney boozer is such a comedy figure that his type has become a well-used property of London vaudeville. But these crazed, maddened, partially poisoned liquor-fiends are not funny at all. On the stage of the Houston Street Winter Garden or the Grand Street Burlesque you will commonly see representations of the Bowery hobo which are very funny. But it is rare to see them shewn under the influence of liquor. They do not make you laugh—they make you turn pale, they sadden you, they afflict you. Maxim Gorky wrote of "Creatures that once were men," or, to translate his title literally, "Those who once were"; but in all the night-lying houses of Nizhni or Moscow he never saw any so abject, so far from their Creator and the Divine Workshop as these.

I go with one to a saloon, just an old-time saloon. There are a dozen or so of them together. The inside reminds me of the opium den of the melodramatic stage, where creatures beyond hope lie moaning in dreadful despair and human abasement. And I sample the drink. The colourless variety might well be gin by its appearance; the coloured looked like recognisable whisky. But what is this stuff? It is not like vodka. It is not fuming mountain liquor, which is often potent enough in all conscience, served in ram's horns, brown, aromatic, brain-suffusing. The first taste is not unpleasant. The first thought is that it is a real drink—the second thought, instinctive and coming up from the stomach and the vitals, is that it is poison. The body sends its alarm signal to the brain. After two glasses you feel poisoned for two days; the nerves of the nose still register from it. The effect is not loquacity, not sociability, but sheer blur. There is little interesting conversation in these places where this moonshine is sold. It kills and yet it creates a craving.

The liquor is cheap. In England, you get what we call "a double whisky" for twenty cents. You can get the same quantity in the Bowery for fifteen. There are places where you can get a drink for a dime. This is cheaper than in most non-Prohibition countries, and I must surmise that the graft is less than the tax would be, so that the American bootlegger, despite the difficulties of his trade, can now undersell the European distiller.

The medicine bottles you see about testify to another source of liquor, and that is the drug store. The derelicts do not carry hip-flasks, for they have only one pocket that will hold anything and that is reached through the mouth. But you see them occasionally with these bottles. If you have the sweet-stuff of Benedictine or the dissolved odour of cognac, certain druggists will supply redistilled, methylated or—well, they have their secrets. Who knows what they will supply! Among many things I admire in America is that ordinance whereby patent medicines are labelled explicitly. The Pure Drugs Act demands that the various panaceas for human ills shall have been analysed and their constituent ingredients publicly declared in print upon the bottles. Now if this were applied to the alcoholic blendings they sell, it might be of considerable public service.

However, I have heard that those who really survive some years of drinking the new stuff do not care for the old, the real and the pure. King Mithridates could not be poisoned because he had cultivated the habit of taking poisons in small doses for many years. Other people's poison was his food. But I imagine there are few Mithridateses on the Bowery—the intestinal ordeal is too great, too violent.

When I was first in New York in the spring of 1913 I was shewn certain interesting types on the southern end of the Bowery, my first visual introduction to "dope fiends." One knew them by their glazed eyes, pallid faces, and shambling gait. Today you do not distinguish these people because those under the influence of bad liquor look that way too. Chinatown has been cleaned up. Hundreds of bad characters have been packed off to China. There is a tacit assumption that there is really no crime in New York's Chinatown. We laugh at those coaches waiting on the Great White Way to take provincials sight-seeing down there. No New Yorker ever takes a seat. He knows that nothing interesting will be shewn. In that he is right. It is the same in Paris and London. Those midnight parties of strangers in *chars-a-bancs* listening to a gabby youth with a loud speaker, seldom have any fun. You cannot see the night life of a city in that way, least of all the life of the Chinese, the most secretive people in the world. But that does not mean that there is not some strange night life in the purlieus of the southern Bowery.

It has been said to me that Chatham Square is only the business capital of the American Chinese, the Wall Street, so to speak,—that while swarms do business there, they go away at night and live uptown at Washington Heights or in the Bronx. But that is not the case; the vast majority of New York Chinese live where their work and profession are.

It is true you never see a drunken Chinaman. If one of the community gets inebriated some others will spirit him away and lay him out on the floor of some back room till he is sober. The Chinese present a very respectable appearance and are easily more discreet, more dignified, and decent than Jews, Irish, or Italians. You see them with their opium pipes, but they are smoking cigars in them—they seem to have turned their swords into pruning-hooks. Go to their characteristic theatres or cinemas, and you see that their taste is refined and even intellectual. They are the highbrows of a burlesque-ridden neighbourhood. And yet I feel that the characteristic Chinese vice does prevail down there and that the immunity of the bootlegger covers the doper as well. Under the bootlegger's umbrella there are some dope-traffickers.

The joy-riders go down for chew mein and visit the Chinese Delmonico with its elaborate inlaid tables and well-served dishes. But the district abounds in queer little resorts where the foreigner, I mean the American, is by no means welcome. I followed one of the most sinister-looking figures on the Bowery one night, a repulsive bent-backed toad-like old man, and he went into a Chinese dive, but I dared not follow him. Early one Sunday morning, however, I went into that place and was, I suspect, served with a drug in my tea. I got into a very exalted state and I realised the appalling danger. In a fit of dejection and melancholy one would naturally return to that dark corner of that cloudy Chinese den and repeat the experiment. It was a curious place. I nursed my head as if I were the worse for drink, but I watched the dreary-faced customers get happy, especially watched some who surrounded a beautiful Chinese young woman in a worshipping group. I missed the whole of my sleep after that and spent the rest of Sunday in a jaded apathetic frame of mind. But I did not return. After all, you never know whether you are potentially a dope fiend, but once you are it is impossible to get back to normal.

But under cover of the new drinking it should be borne in mind that there may be considerable drug taking. And the disrespect of the law obvious in the open saloons is likely to make every one cynical about illegalities. Obedience to law is wrought in the mind; but if that mental discipline is lacking, who knows what may be conceived? The concomitants of the alcohol vice are other more secret vices. It is not easy for the casual visitor or outsider to find out what goes on behind closed doors—but without being of an unduly suspicious turn of mind, I feel that there is a good deal going on behind the Bowery—a good deal that is curious, to say the least.

But there is a pleasant feature of the Bowery. There are few women drunkards. The women, like the Chinese, seem to be taken care of. I was walking with a young lady one night, and we took a fancy to a respectable hobo and befriended him. He said he came from New Orleans, but he mistook the appearance of my friend, who was all that a charming lady should be.

"Ah, my dear," said he, "you have a bad time

here with the cops, don't you? But in N'Orleans a girl can walk up and down and choose her partner and never be interfered with." Apparently he did not approve the sex calm of the Bowery.

I was often in those restaurants where you get a sort of supper for eight cents and there saw not a few derelict women. The proprietors are friendly, give them a cup of coffee and some scraps of food and let them bide. There at the tables they collapse and sleep till dawn. They always melt when a man treats them to a slice of apple pie, and begin to talk of what was once their homes, of lost husbands, lost children. They are the lost old women of New York, and very unlike the lost old women of London who are so beer-stricken.

Yes, the Bowery is a strange, haunting, haunted street. I walk all the way down and then all the way back. It holds me. I am in a subterranean passage, and the gay bright New York with its never-dying gaiety and movement is far above, in the night air, in the night sky, denting heaven with its towers. It is a serene spectacle to look out over New York from the top of the Woolworth Building at night; and you think you see the city. That is the zenith, up there where Orion is striding by. But the nadir is the Bowery. Down there you have also a true perspective of the city, and I think I know more of New York because of the many nights I have spent there.

CHAPTER XIX

From the Flop House Door

I WENT into the Flop House one night shortly after twelve and found that the Mission Service was still going on. The room was full, and some men were standing at the back. I squeezed into a seat beside an old collarless derelict. A rubicund and benevolent gentleman was addressing the meeting, and over his head the electric sign, JESUS SEES, was burning. There were no women in the audience, but two women missionaries were seated in front beside the harmonium and the black cross. I think there were a few professional *savees* in the congregation, respectable men who go habitually to meetings of this kind, habitually get saved and testify. The derelicts waiting, standing in the doorway, hoped to get their seats when the meeting closed and they went home. They waited for the saved to go home in order to get a "flop" for the night. But other drunks, less like foolish virgins, had got there in good time and found their place for the night. They held their aching heads in their hands and stared downward.

"What a wonderful dinner I had to-night, boy," says the portly missionary. "I met a friend uptown and we went to a good restaurant and we had just everything a man could want. We had beautiful thick red tomato soup. It was real hot, just the thing on a cold night. Then we had clams, so daintily fried, like poetry. I could have made my

FLOP HOUSE
Creatures that once were men live under the city in the Bowery.

whole supper on clams alone. Then we had corn and yams and roast turkey, hot corn and butter, and I thought, 'See how the good Lord rewards his servants.' Wonderful turkey. I thought of you poor men down here and I asked myself—'Why don't they share in all this?' Then I remembered our brother Peters and his story, how he was once on the bum, hadn't a shirt, and how he saw the light one night. And, oh, the difference! Oh, the difference! Isn't that so, brother? Praise God! Praise God!"

The missionary began a long prayer, never disturbed by the splashing of water at the back of the room. I noticed men get up now and then, stagger towards the doorway, and then return to their seats, and as I was perplexed by the splashing I peeped round to see what was causing it. Then I saw that there was a tap at the back of the room, and that the drunks, crazed by thirst, kept going to it to moisten their lips and their throats.

A woman missionary told the men how God had been especially kind to her and to them that day. She had nearly been in a taxi-accident on Forty-second Street. It was so near. She might have been killed. Think of that! And they would have lost their sister. They ought specially to thank God that night that she had been saved.

The benevolent missionary, rubber-tyred, rotund, with apple cheeks and round rimmed spectacles, came down the aisle with elastic step. To a forlorn drunk in front of me he put the question—"Have you found Jesus?"

"Noah," he howled.

"Then take the air!" said the missionary.

"Have you found Jesus?" he asked of me.

"Yes," I said.

"Praise God. Won't you come forward and testify?"

"I'd rather remain at the back."

But various young men testified till nearly two o'clock. This was a night of wrestling with the unregenerate East Side. The saved testified; the unsaved snored. There was a hymn, another prayer, and then, blessed relief, the Doxology.

As the old harmonium steamed forth "Praise God from Whom all blessings flow," the orderly at the back seemed to come to life, and striding among the seats lifted the sleeping and incapable by the arms to drooping and standing positions.

"All up! All up!" he shouted, like a corporal. "Praise Him, ye creatures here below—all up, all up!"

So the creatures that once were men struggled to attention and wavered during the lingering Amen. Then the "Jesus Sees" electric sign went out, and the missionaries went home, and the other lights were extinguished, and in the dark the ragged congregation settled down to sleep. The Mission had gone; the flop remained.

I vacated my seat and gave it to one of the homeless, and I went out into the street to see what happened to those who were too late and couldn't get a shelter for the night. The orderly was there haranguing the blear-eyed.

"I'll help no man that's hit the booze," he kept saying.

A ragged fellow lifted his shirt to show me wounds got in France—"Say, ain't they worth a quarter? Come on, gimme a quarter for a flop. I'll ship in the morning and get out of all this."

I said to him: "You're very drunk. You'd better go somewhere and sober off. In the morning go and get a cup of coffee and a sandwich. You'll need it."

I gave him a dime—five cents less than the price of a drink. "Gawd bless you!" said he. He evidently thought I had been inside testifying. "Gawd bless you!" and off he went to try and make up the deficiency of five cents for another drink.

I went into the Mission Room again—all was dark. All the sleepers were bowed as in prayer. There was a terrible gloom and depression as one might feel on the first night in a Leper hospital.

When I came out again I fell in with a strange-looking fellow who by his tawny face and Oriental eyes seemed to be Chinese—a great rarity, a drunken Chinaman.

"Why's your face so red?" I asked. "Have you come off a ship?" He grinned at me, but he was friendly.

"I'm an Indian," he answered.

"What, a Hindoo?"

"No. Come off a reservation in Maine."

"Oh, a Red Indian."

"I come from railway camp on the Grand Central. I've got money but can't touch it yet. I'm looking for some one would buy my coat."

He smelt strongly of alcohol but he was not tipsy. He had been too proud or too sober to take a seat inside the flop house and pretended he wanted money on his coat so as to go to a hotel. To-morrow he would be able to redeem it.

Extraordinary, wavering, blind-eyed, white-faced drunks came floundering toward the door of the flophouse, and the orderly waved them off. They walked in the uncertain way of contrary cows being driven to a shed by a boy with a stick. The Indian grinned his disdain. The boss relit his cigar-stump and looked the other way.

This Indian and I went for a walk in Chinatown. So we turned in Doyer Street and at a step left the grim realism of the Bowery, the subterranean Bowery, for it is like a sort of mine-way of which Third Avenue is the shaft, and you might expect to see blind pit ponies come scampering along. It is a misery mine. At a step we left it and were in Fairyland, narrow romantic Doyer Street hung with exaggerated, illuminated medal-ribbons, peopled by squint-eyed Easterners. The Red Indian seemed curiously to be at home in Doyer Street among the Chinese. He belonged.

His main idea was to take me to a place where

I could get him a drink, and with that in view we climbed the stairs of a Chinese Club. There were columns of Chinese characters on the walls, but the place did not seem to be open to the public. Two Chinamen were sitting on the stairs, halfway up, smoking long opium pipes with cigars in them. In the gloom they perhaps thought the Indian one of themselves, and we got by, and we came to a broad ill-lit upper room with terra-cotta blinds and big square inlaid tables, and a large number of Chinese talking in low voices, smoking and gambling. But we had hardly got our noses inside this den when we were assailed by an extremely husky fellow who gave the Indian a shove which would have sent him flying down stairs, but that I saved him. The heavy-curtained doors were then shut in our faces and deliberately bolted.

"There is a bar, I know," said the Indian morosely. "Sure to be open if I could get a landscape on it."

I found that the Indian knew the East Side pretty well, but he knew none of the names of the streets. He judged where he was by the contours of the houses and kept adjusting his direction by the "slant on the Elevated." We visited several bars which proved to be shut as it was after two a.m., and the ordinary poor dives close up about that time. Still the Indian thought he would find another if he could get "a landscape on it."

At last we came to "Louey's Lunch." Let me call it that. It had a three-o'clock-in-the-morning air. Some men were lying in the sawdust on the floor; men seated lay forward with their heads on dreary stone-topped tables. Some men were moaning weirdly; they thought they were singing. Others were engaged in drunken argument.

We went to the bar and the Indian had a glass of Scotch and I a bottle of beer. The two drinks cost thirty cents. I took mine to a table and sat down; the Indian gulped his and retreated to a room at the back. Presently he returned, drew a chair to my knees and, looking up in my face, whispered confidentially, "I didn't think I could hold it."

He drew a finger across his brow and struck off the perspiration, for he was bathed in sweat.

"I don't know what it is, but ever since my house burned down las' year, I sweat."

"Your house burned down?"

"Yes. I was living with a white woman up there near Augusta. We bought a seven-hundred-dollar piano and next day the house burn down. Nothing saved. Only a nigger cat."

"The nigger cat?"

"Yes, she came out all right. Good cat. Been offered twenty-five bucks for her. Tail as long as your arm. My daughter Doris put the cat in a bag and we set off for Lewiston."

"Hey, boy, give an old twice-ruptured man room to stretch his legs."

We were interrupted by a fussy fellow who was trying to arrange an old man's body on a couple of rickety chairs. The Indian sniggered.

"He calls me boy. Heugh! Ye can't tell an Indian's age."

My companion looked about twenty-five or even less, with his cloth cap pulled down over his red childish brow. It was a surprise to learn he was forty-seven and had a grown daughter, Doris, now lost on the streets of New York.

"Yes, she put the cat in a bag and we pulled out from Augusta in a freighter. I had a friend on the train. But thirty miles out we looked at the bag and saw the cat had escaped. There was deep snow on the track and we were waiting, so I got out and looked for traces. What you think? That nigger cat got back home and was found in the burned-out house and she never left a footmark. We asked a motor man to look—thirty miles and not a mark. That nigger cat walked the irons the whole way."

No one in the saloon gave any heed to us. We had a long quiet talk. The Indian spoke in a whisper all the while, and I had to put my ear down to him to hear what he had to say. There was a big bully striding about the place now. He had bushy white whiskers, a beetle-brimmed hat, and a dirty red rosette in his button-hole. He was fat and had a fat sagging face—the type of a rough guy in a movie burlesque. Whenever any one put down anything for a drink he sang in a maudlin voice—

> "I love the dear silver which shi-ines,"

or

> "Meet me to-night in a dream!"

The boss of the establishment was not behind the bar, but walked about and kept a watchful eye on the door or on the customers.

He was a clean-cut athletic-looking fellow, neatly dressed and active. But his face lacked the milk of human kindness. It was acid, and his eyes were deliberately half-closed like those of an enraged cat.

"Hi, you!" said he to the bully—"Ye seem to think ye're running this joint. Take a walk. Say! Take the air!"

The Indian looked up at me and whispered, "I know that feller. We Indians never forget faces. He's a Gawd-damned son of a . . . He'd as soon hit you over the head with that stick as anything. Just wait. I'll go up and ask him a question. See if he doesn't recognise me."

He crept up to the coat-tails of the swaggering hobo and murmured to him—

"D'ye know Jed Tyler the turnkey's lookin' for ye!"

The old man turned and gave him a knowing wink which distorted the whole of one side of his awful face and answered something. The Indian, content, came smiling back to me.

"Last time I saw him he was in Augusta jail. I handed him a hacksaw hidden in a loaf of bread," said he.

The boss was visibly losing patience. He strode up to the man who was now leaning against the bar and flourishing his stick.

"Look here, if you've got the money for a drink pay it down," said he. "If not, get out. Twenty cents, not a dime. If you've got fifteen, put it down. Nothing for ten cents. Put it down and get a drink. Not got it? Then get out! Take a walk, take a walk!"

And with that he caught the old man behind and gave him what is known in the Bowery as "the bum's rush," push, bang, thump, kick, from bar to doorway out into the air and the street.

It was well done, and it won my respect. That dark young man should go far.

The Indian said he knew a place where the liquor was better. If I liked he'd shew me, only it was an eel-pot.

"An eel-pot?" I enquired.

"Oh, you wouldn't know what that is. Well, a cat shop."

We went out and the Indian, eyeing the line of the tops of houses, began to get his bearings for the eel-pot.

"It's near a little park," said he. "I was sleeping in a doorway one night and the boss came out and asked me if I'd like to earn five dollars.

'Sure,' said I. I went in at a side door, down steps, and into the kitchen to wash dishes. Say, there's lots of fine girls in there!"

The Indian paused and thought of girls with gusto.

It was now three-thirty, and the East Side groaned in heavy sleep while somnambulist figures slouched homelessly and unhappily along the littered street. The park of which the Indian spoke proved to be that stone enclosure at the head of Delancey Street and in it were a score of miserable derelicts huddled together sleeping.

In a back street near the Grand Burlesque there were a number of cars waiting amid the litter and garbage, and we came to a cellar-way over which were scrawled the words: ENTERTAINMENT: SONGS IN ALL LANGUAGES. We essayed an entrance. But the door-keeper could not admit us. "Full up to-night, boys. Come another night."

The Indian was disappointed but accepted the decision. I made a note to come again another night and find out what was going on.

Night was giving way to dawn when we resumed our wanderings. Newspaper vans had dumped bales of the morning papers on the pavement beside the not yet opened news counters on the corners of the main road, and men with sleep-infested eyes were uncording them.

A curious thing now happened. I had thought the Indian penniless. He wasn't. He stood me a drink.

We came to one of those white-painted glaring little shops where they sell "Orange Drink" all night.

"Would ye like a glass of tonic?" asked the Indian. I agreed, and he displayed a quarter.

"Wherever did you get that?" I asked. "I thought you were broke."

"Old Charlie slipped it me," said he, referring to the old fellow whom he had recognised from Augusta jail.

So we each drank that yellow medicinal wash which is so popular in New York. The cost was a dime, and my Indian received fifteen cents change. I felt he stood treat with a good deal of dignity.

It was the tribal tradition of exchanging presents. He was at great pains to let me know that he was not a beggar, and though it is true he had gone down under the influence of what is called civilisation he still preserved some trace of good character.

He told me his wife was working in a shop in Boston, but he was reserved about his daughter Doris. Doris was in New York and he pretended he did not know where, but I am afraid she is a dancing girl in some East Side resort and has gone down in her way as her father has in his.

We walked and talked till dawn, halting at various surprising places, one of which was called The Moscow Village Inn, whose window is like a decorated Christmas tree in a slum parlour, for the street in which it is found is one of the most dreary lanes behind the Bowery. And we stopped at the swagger Fountain of Joy. Outside stood a magnificent Packard which must have cost ten thousand dollars. Then we went into an all-night restaurant where the Indian said he had often bummed a cup of coffee free, and we had sandwiches and coffee for eight cents. Then we proceeded to Fulton Market and sat ourselves with men with fish-scales in their hair at the great fish-market bar, seated under a carved ceiling and facing the mahogany grandeur of what was once a substantial saloon, now deserted to the soul-warming splendour of great gleaming coffee-urns.

Perhaps the night did not end in vain for the Indian. I made him a small present and at the same time he stood in a fair way of getting a job shifting and stacking up empty herring tubs.

His real trade was that of "spiker," which he had learned at Hallowell, Maine. We parted at dawn. I said to him, "I have always heard there were two sorts of Indians—Good Injun and Bad Injun. I have come to the conclusion that you're a Good Injun and I wish you luck. Get back to your job and keep off the drink. Good-bye."

He looked at me demurely through the corners of his eyes as I mounted the El. stairs to go home.

CHAPTER XX

A Speakeasy Under the Sky

THEY told me of a new speakeasy on the top of a high Fifth Avenue building. I was invited to the opening on the first night, a quiet domestic affair, just the bootlegger's friends. Pat and I had been dancing; we came in about half past eleven one Saturday night. The coloured boy working the elevator took up to the roof without a word. Did he know by our eyes where we were going? Or was the rest of the house occupied only by day? We shot up several floors. "One flight up to walk," said the lift-boy laconically, pointing to the stairway.

It was facing Madison Square Garden, a roof-runway with attic-rooms extending from Fifth Avenue to the next street, a distance of some two hundred feet. A young Irishman and his wife are at home to his thirsty well-wishers. He has been in partnership hitherto with his brothers who have a bar in the "roaring Forties"; now he is starting on his own. The drinks are the same but the premises are novel. He should have great success in the hot summer months and perhaps indicate a way to utilise the many terraces and recesses on the steeps of the new high buildings of New York.

The air is fresh and there is a marvellous exhilaration as one walks the roof. One is standing above New York, above business, above the law. Pat and I asked for bacardis and were brought as well a long drink of "velvet." There was a ruddy Virginia ham and the proprietor's wife brought us some of that too. That was hospitality; all drinks and all food were "on the house" this first night. Next time we come in everything will cost a dollar. It will be worth the money for the air and the view alone. You stand facing the immense tower of the Metropolitan Building, almost *vis-à-vis* the great lighted clock. Far down below like mechanical toys on a floor you see the swarm of traffic, the tiny cabs lighted some with two lights, some with three, some with four or five lights, threading their way in the confluence of streets where Broadway and the Avenues meet. The streets like dark canals wander away northward out of vision. It is not a gay part of New York. The garden with its little lights and its little monument where the annual Christmas tree is lit on Christmas Eve is an island of life on which darkness is encroaching. It reminded me curiously of the Zocalo in Mexico City, the dim vast square of the pyramid of the God of War. Except for a certain effulgence among the stars you could not surmise the existence of the Great White Way twenty streets away.

No music has yet been brought to the speakeasy, but for sheer gaiety we sang our own song and danced on the roof. Then it was midnight. We stood and watched the clock which tells half New York the time. On the assumption that most of the city slept the clock had ceased chiming; the face darkened, the red light appeared, the beacon on the apex of the tower flashed twelve times. Few people down below looked up. One does not need to look so high to see the time. We felt for a moment like astrologers on a lonely lighthouse observing some celestial portent.

"We are going to put up awnings," said the boss. "We know we shall succeed; we do not want a crowd of people, we could not handle a crowd if we had it. What we want is nice people; you know what I mean. We don't want men and women who will try to push one another off the roof or get into such a condition that they throw up over the parapet."

I think the place ought to become a rendezvous for musicians and poets and brilliant actresses. The stars of New York ought to meet the stars of the New York sky. This speakeasy is another illustration of what Prohibition is doing for drinking.

CHAPTER XXI

Theodor and the Ritz-Carlton Roof

YOU must be known to Theodor. A smile from him, a nod of recognition as you enter the Ritz-Carlton show that socially you "belong." He is the Theodor; you must enter by him.

Theodor Szarvas is the clever head-waiter. Under him are the black-coated captains, under them are the white-coated waiters, and under all are the guests. Like most famous head-waiters he is an international personality. The sentry does not present arms when he passes Buckingham Palace but the waiters salute when he enters the Carlton Hotel. He is a Hungarian, speaks French for preference and is equally well-known at Paris, Vienna, Monte Carlo. He once ran a luxurious establishment in the Schwarzwald; it had a mountain stream running through it, a restaurant with a natural brook dividing the floorway. But that was in the romantic days before the war.

Theodor is slight, velvety, elastic. As he advances or retreats, conducting his guests among the tables he has something of the spring and poise of a fencer. His face is slashed by experience, but nervous and sensitive, his eyes observant. He is a rare head-waiter; he is ascetic. The choicest food in America is at his disposal, but his body measurements are below normal. He looked to me like the new type of administrative official who had risen to high position through untiring energy and persistence.

Fashion journalists go regularly to the Ritz to note the modes. It is a very charmingly designed oval-ceilinged, octagonal-walled restaurant. If you sit in the centre facing the entrance it seems as if there were a Spanish patio beyond it and from this patio the guests perpetually rise to greet Theodor in the gracious archway on the threshold. Back of the arriving guests the orchestra is playing invisibly. Business men with relaxed expressions on their faces come in with discreetly, simply and expensively dressed women. Rich young idlers come in with slim sylph-like society girls. You observe the polo-player type of youth with the gloss of Harvard still on his brow. Theodor, who is a respectful major-domo to the elderly and pompous, is more like a pet uncle to the young ones. Without touching him they seem to cling to him as he leads them along. No one tips him openly; that would be too much, but every one prizes his rare smile. I was told he was on the pay-roll of half the wealthy men of New York. They do not slip notes into his hand but they "take care" of him and in return he takes care of them and of members of their families when they appear at the Ritz, see that they get good tables and that they are treated with the dignity due to their wealth and position. It means a great deal to be able to arrive at the Ritz with the aplomb and suave manner of one who knows that he is at home, a habitué and a patron.

Theodor invited me to the opening of the Japanese Roof Garden and I promised to come with my partner Helen, and dance. "I should think you dance very nicely yourself?" I ventured.

"No, I deny myself that," he replied. "But I dance at home with my wife and you should see how our children laugh at us."

The Ritz Roof is on the first floor; there are ten floors above it. Is that not quaint? Commercially it has proved more profitable to have the roof indoors and near the street. Is that more "sophistication"? It reminds me of an artificial sea-side resort where dogs did not bark at night and cocks did not salute the morn.

Nevertheless it must be said that the Japanese Roof Garden of the Ritz-Carlton does produce the illusion of being on the top of the building. It is a large marquee, apparently of canvas, striped green and yellow, and it is banked on three sides with scarlet flowers. Red-backed chairs and the red dresses of some ladies, and rouged cheeks heightened the general red effect.

Helen and I arrived on the opening night about eight o'clock. There was a noise and a bustle like the same on the first night on a liner when all manner of brilliant strangers are confusedly entering. Out of doors the rain was streaming down; on the whole it was lucky the Roof was not a roof and that the West wind had no power to trouble tempestuously the marquee.

"Let me take charge of your distinguished hat," said Theodor.

We were given a table advantageously situated for seeing the assemblage of guests. This perhaps appealed more to Helen than to me. I ate my *poussin paysanne* but Helen fed also on dresses. Her eyes lingered on golden brocades, interwoven with blue and vermilion threads; on a lithe sword-like woman in a scabbard of rhinestones and white silk; on a lady in a coatee of black glass with a green bouquet on the shoulder. Helen said the coatee was a blouse and that the close-strung black glass beads were sequins. "My dear," said I, "sequins are coins, and blouses are not worn at night," but Helen's face remained inattentively vague.

The only males who seemed to be wearing full evening dress were Charlie Chaplin and some of the superior waiters. All were in dinner-jackets. In the lapels of their tuxedos they wore flowers, cornflowers, carnations, roses. Jewels were profuse. On all hands we saw women handcuffed to wealth with bracelets, haltered with pearls. The men looked much more interesting than the women. Clever heads abounded. The men were stockbrokers, lawyers, financial operators, sharpers, but all splendidly successful ones, winners at the dollar-collecting game. The women were creatures of leisure and pleasure who were there to spend what the men earned. There were no hard-faced professional women, no women with hunted faces, but plenty of the pampered and the pretty. The men handled them with an air of proprietorship, handled them so much more than they would have dared to do in English society, feeling their fat arms as they passed their chairs. Indulgent demoiselles came and sat on daddy's knee and fondled his neck. Their was plenty of liquor. Waiters with champagne-buckets trundled around. It seemed out of keeping with the wealth of the assembly to see a party united around a large straw-covered bottle of Chianti . . . ah, but real Chianti! There were lots of bottles among the legs of the guests endangering almost priceless gowns and not a few upsets, though nobody seemed to care.

The dancing was very boisterous. "Harlem translated into diamonds," I called it. These men who know how to make money are very individualistic. They kick, they bump, they think only of their gorgeous selves. These *femmes de luxe* think only how lovely they look and how satisfying or unsatisfying their partners.

Helen and I sipped our delicious Cerise Melba and then joined the dancing crush. Most discreet and charming of all the dancers was Charlie Chaplin, who two-stepped along the wall with his face to it as if afraid to be seen. The greying popular idol with light-dazzled face and fruity Jewish smile bore on his arm an elderly woman, no naughty screen-star but some pleasant aunt. We liked him. The wealth and fashion of New York were there, but it was he who made the gala memorable.

CHAPTER XXII

The Burning of the Netherland Tower

ONE night we were on our way to Paul Whiteman's to dance and our attention was arrested by a group of star-gazers on the corner of Sixth Avenue and 48th Street. They were looking high North East to a conflagration in the sky. A fire-engine went roaring by with exultant tremulous clamour. We went over to the best corner and stared with the others. Far away in the sky there was what appeared to us like a tall ship burning on top of a skyscraper, an uplifted bonfire gleaming, candling, under the fading stars. A train passing on the elevated railway hid the strange sight from view, and then restored it to vision. We thought it was St. Patrick's cathedral for there was a dark tower silhouetted against the light of the flames. It was a marvellously thrilling sight, dramatic, ritualistic, awe-inspiring. We clung to one another in hushed excitement. The traffic of New York lumbered multitudinously in all directions, cabs with theatre parties slid astream the cross-streets like timber toppling forward on a spring flood, the intervening elevated trains with illuminated moving windows and accompanying grind of wheels incessantly roared by, deafening and excluding. But the celestial phenomenon remained: New York had lit an altar in the heavens or the heavens had opened and some one was coming down—perhaps Elisha descending in the same way as he went up.

It was not St. Patrick's; the crowd put us right. Some one identified the building and every one who knew New York agreed that he was right. "It is the Plaza Annex." A new-comer gave more exact intelligence: "It is the new Netherland Tower, all floors alight above the twenty-third. The fire broke out on the thirty-eighth floor."

Visitors to New York in 1927 must have admired the new buildings which had arisen, over against the Plaza at the entrance to Central Park, the Netherland lofty, severe, mitred, like some North German mediæval tower, magnified and exalted to the stars, and beside it the less lofty but not less beautiful Savoy-Plaza in Italian style, looking like the macrocosm of a Savoy tower.

One stood in the park at night-fall and marvelled. The Plaza bed-room windows lighting up in hundreds, the tiers of irregular light and shade make one think of all humanity living in one building. It is surely one of the most moving sights of New York and I have known Englishmen who made the pilgrimage to that part of the city several times a week just to see the Plaza and New York light up for the night. And there was added to that spectacle the greyness and simplicity of the Netherland Tower and the closely-neighbouring Savoy-Plaza, as yet unlighted, un-lived in, candidates waiting for confirmation in the community of Manhattan.

Skyscrapers do not burn. One does not expect to see the Woolworth or the Paramount Building

BURNING OF THE NETHERLAND TOWER
Fifth Avenue one night had a great candle in the sky.

on fire at any time. Nearly all the fires of New York are in the old houses. That was a reason why this beacon was such a thrilling spectacle.

The first alarm was given at half-past eight, the second followed right away. Third, fourth and fifth alarms were given. I imagine the excitement among the reporters at Police Headquarters. The press representatives rushed to the scene and arrived hard upon the engines.

Patricia and I having dined at Paul Whiteman's in the spacious gloom which possesses night clubs during the theatre hours, returned to the scene of the fire, walking up Fifth Avenue. New York was streaming that way, all heads uplifted towards the high altar of fire. The great avenue was Oriental with fire-worshippers.

A hater of modern civilisation once quoted Shakespeare charmingly to me with reference to the avenue. Loathing it as a monument of success yet admiring the red and blue lights of the signal-towers, he said it reminded him of adversity—"which like a toad ugly and venomous bears yet a precious jewel in its brow." This night it bore the Kohinoor.

Curious that something which is purely destructive like a fire should make one feel so exhilarated! The people on the avenue marched forward as if accompanied by military bands. The fiery sign which drew them on grew in power as we got nearer it. The falling waves of sparks became visible. We began to see the flaming poles and red glowing beams which parting from the main edifice gyrated and planed downward, looking at times like flaming assegais hurtled at an unseen foe.

The crowds were banked up at 57th and 58th and 59th Streets. The whole platform in front of the Plaza Hotel was occupied. There were crowds in Central Park. It was a magnificent place for seeing a fire. There was an open-air theatre for the show. The best places were those on the fountain facing the building.

A United States flag had surmounted the tower, blown about by the wind in flaming tatters and shreds. It moved every one as if reminding of the American anthem and the Star-Spangled Banner above the flames of burning Baltimore.

Acosta and Chamberlain in their great Bellanca plane, attracted by the conflagration came droning over from the Roosevelt field where they were engaged in an attempt to establish a new-world record for sustained flight, their red and green lights suggesting a new celestial portent and giving one of the great thrills of the night. The noise of the engines was swallowed up in the uproar of combustion. The machine circled three or four times about the blazing tower and then swept away to the Hudson river sky.

After eleven the theatre crowds began to arrive in private cars and taxis. Fifth Avenue became glutted with vehicles which the police were busily diverting. There was a parade of fashionable people and society journalists might well have been at work noting personalities and dresses. Women in low-cut evening gowns stood in rows gazing upward, all as it were posed for a photograph, their faces white and still and suffused with light. The mayor himself, drenched to the skin with fire-spray, stood ahead of the mass of onlookers, watching the operations of the helpless fire-brigade. The guests of the Plaza whose windows faced the tower gazed sleeplessly outward; the thousands in Central Park gazed spellbound; the group that had taken possession of the fountain seemed changed to a mass of unmoving drab statuary. From every roof and vantage-ground of the city people gazed and wondered. They looked across from 110th Street and Harlem and the Bronx. Commuters stared from the suburbs and from New Jersey towns.

But those who like Patricia and myself were directly underneath, had the great living picture of the fire. The height of the building was entirely out of reach of the water. In a helpless impotent way the long curve of hose-water faded downward and jetted the twenty-third storey. The down-dropping, curvetting incandescent poles meeting the stream of water in mid-air performed surprisingly, jumping, dancing or even revolving as if spun.

On the twentieth floor of the Savoy-Plaza the firemen were at work having hoisted a hose to that height. But presumably there was not enough pressure to force the water higher. The Netherland and the Savoy were joined at this height by a grey arc of water looking like a colourless rainbow.

How every one's neck ached looking up! Yet one must continue looking. Each moment we expected to see the whole upper part of the tower come tumbling down. That chance really made it dangerous to remain where we were. But our neighbours and ourselves were too fascinated to move back to a sheltered position. The top of the tower did not fall. Apparently the main structure of steel and brick was not being very much affected by the heat and the flame. What was burning was the elaborate scaffolding of the tower which was in course of construction. At times neighbouring roofs seemed to have caught, but these little fires were speedily extinguished; at times the twenty-third floor below the tower seemed to be well alight, the windows belching forth volumes of black smoke. The walls of the building proved to be indestructible. There were some moments of subdued awe and fear and one was when a considerable portion of the West side fell away, flaming and roaring through the night-air. This caused a general expectation of a spread of the fire but as a matter of fact it helped to diminish the blaze. The new fires it started were speedily put out. All that happened was that the statue of General Sherman came under fire once more; it had been bombarded all the night. Sparks also started fires in some automobiles.

No one was killed in the fire: I believe no one was injured. The loss was covered by insurance. Every one had something to talk about; lovers were united by the thrill; foes forgot their quarrel. The fire went on all night. The crowds remained fascinated, unable to tear themselves away. Seldom has a fire been so well arranged, so much enjoyed. New York was made one in the fire light.

CHAPTER XXIII

Mountain Scenery

THE great shadowy Savoy-Plaza and Sherry-Netherland are sheer cliffs. The Ritz Tower with bright glimmering obelisk surmounting it is like a cliff with a hydro on the top of it. This is a grand part of New York. Above the Heckscher Building like a snow-crest gleams its silvery coronet, globe and bird. Fifth Avenue is like the military road to Persia and at this point leaves a great range and debouches on to the Steppes. From Central Park one looks back upon all the mountains, their glittering peaks and shadowy heights.

Going along 59th Street one approaches lofty mountains; they are the sentinel rocks at 59th and Broadway, General Motors and Fisk Buildings. They stand as it were at the entrance to a deep ravine, some Gorge of Dariel in New York; a national pass at which battles might be fought. At this majestic pass commences the most spectacular walk in the city. It is a much better approach to the supreme grandeur of Broadway than from down-town. The view is marvellous. Far in the distance and going right up into the sky, like Popocatepetl or Kazbek are the terraced heights of the Paramount. And leading up to it are tier upon tier of lights, Arcadia, China View, Paul Whiteman's, the Gaiety with blazoned *King of Kings,* and the Astor Roof with its dim torches.

As you walk down Broadway the splendour increases and the Times Building comes into view behind. Broadway becomes broader to flow concurrently with Seventh Avenue. Rivulets and cascades of light dazzle the eyes. Here is Tamara's castle, red porphyry rocks, a fast-rushing stream and the murmur of eternity. There are caves and dukhans and bandits and smugglers and wild flowers. And in an exhilaration which you feel amid a tumultuous upheaval of Nature you come to the Times Building and what has been felicitously called the "Cross Roads of the World."

CHAPTER XXIV

Tough Audiences

WHEN a play has run for some time and has been accepted as a successful piece the tough audiences begin to appear. These are the audiences who have just heard of it and have been told that it is very good. This does not so much apply to musical comedy as to witty and original plays. All musical comedy audiences are tender. But there are only a thousand witty people in New York and perhaps ten thousand who honestly appreciate wit. The "wise cracks" of the first few weeks do not all continue to provide mirth.

I saw *Broadway* shortly after it was produced and again five months later and I was much struck by the difference. The first time I saw it from the orchestra stalls, the second time from the stage. Mr. Jed Harris, the lively young brilliant producer, was very eager to let me see night-life dramatised and I have to thank him for these opportunities.

The second occasion was especially interesting. Helen and I were given seats at the cabaret table back scenes. For one night we represented the guests of the Paradise Night Club and were an integral part of the play. At various points in the drama the doors of the night club are thrown open and a corner of the interior becomes visible to the people in the theatre. The audience stared at the half-naked girls prancing out to the fast-beating jazz of, "I love my baby. My baby loves me."

HELEN

MILT
GROSS

And it peered curiously at us sitting in the glamour of an illuminated rose with our ginger-ale concomitants of gin. They had the illusion that we were life and we had the illusion that the audience was art.

A studious girl stood facing the folding doors with a religious book in her hands. This had nothing to do with the play but her only task during the evening was to fling open the doors when the cue came. Intent on not wasting her time she stood there with bowed head, still as a statue, with the big book open on the palms of her hands like some character in a mystery-play. The action proceeded beyond the doors. We listened to the dialogue and to the occasional murmurs of the audience. Then suddenly at a given signal the girl closed the book and took hold of the rope which caused the doors to fly back.

And there was the audience, many-headed, myriad-eyed. Their eyes were converged upon a narrow stage, but ours were opened upon a vast concourse. New York was dramatised for us in them. "But it is a tough audience," said one of the actors, "they only get half the jokes." Still half the thrills was enough. They felt they had a good time. The atmosphere of the night club so admirably reproduced was a novelty to them, obviously only a few of them had ever been in any place of the kind. I realised that the millions of New York lead quiet lives; it is only the thousands who have the gay time.

Jed Harris, who gave us tickets also for his *Spread Eagle* production with its more intellectual audience, is one of the most remarkable young men in the theatrical life of modern New York, a sort of electric man, who overtakes himself in his own conversation and talks in the rapid-fire style employed in his plays. Helen went to draw him. She met Milt Gross at his apartment and he caricatured the producer at the same time. The two impressions of the electric man seemed to supplement one another and so I give them here.

Another night Patricia and I went to see *White Wings* and again to *Rio Rita.* The play and the comedy were both mediocre in quality, but the audiences were much the same, tired and jaded, in office clothes. Pat was beautifully dressed and I was in evening clothes, but we were like a patch of new silk on something inchoate and drab. The only memory of the people we retained was that of sitting behind charming "Lipstick" of the "New Yorker," and she also seemed as if New York did not matter very much.

I went with Helen to the Opera. We saw *Pelias and Melisande,* and of course I was much interested to have an impression of the audience inside the vast Metropolitan Opera House. But except in the horse-shoe of the boxes it was not dressed for the evening. In no opera house in the world would one see such a dowdy audience in the stalls. It is grand opera, they pay ten dollars a seat and they come in office clothes. One may read in this devotion to culture, but I felt it rather to be servitude to culture. Maeterlinck and Debussy are a fatal combination. The opera is romantic, sentimental, unreal. It is very old-fashioned and contrary to the spirit of the modern world, but because it is accepted as culture the audience sits as if hypnotised. Melisande dies for half an hour in an atmosphere of indescribable tedium, but the audience in sheer despite of its own sophisticated up-to-date point of view forces itself to believe that it is appreciating it and enjoying it. It is true that a couple next to us were engaged in quiet facetiousness the whole evening, they were a redeeming feature, they saw the play in a funny light and were able to enjoy it as a satire on sentimentalism.

After the opera we danced till three in the morning at the Mirador Club and what a change that was! All the women were charmingly gowned and the men in evening dress. The elegance which belonged to the opera was given to dance. The barometer stood higher and our spirits went up. Mirador and not Maeterlinck expressed the true spirit of New York.

Patricia received tickets for the pre-first night of Cecil de Mille's *King of Kings.* Critics, journalists and swarms of people interested in the production were invited. De Mille had such success with the *Ten Commandments* that he felt obliged to follow it with a screen version of the life of Christ. Miss MacPherson was nominally responsible for the film version of the Gospel, but some one with theological acumen must have been employed to cut out any part that might offend any particular creed, its interest being made as universal as possible for purely commercial ends. Some people will receive a spiritual message while looking at it. I have no doubt that in some places it may be reverently shown. But this first night was cynical, Bohemian and irreligious. It was curious to me; they sat through it without a laugh, as if they would have been afraid to have been detected laughing. Yet there were some very funny pictures in it. The scene in which St. Matthew comes to Christ and asks him whether he has paid his taxes is of that sort. Christ in reply tells St. Peter to go and cast a line. St. Peter goes fishing in a matter-of-fact way and draws in a fish with apparently a couple of fifty-cent pieces fixed in its mouth. There is no doubt that this as shown on the screen is excruciatingly funny. It ought either to make you laugh or make you angry. The Christian of to-day can try to imitate his Master in some ways, but obviously he cannot fish with the success of St. Peter. The audience however passed it without a smile. "This is something too holy for mirth," it seemed to say. Our neighbours frowned at us for laughing. Then we saw Mary Magdalene purified and Lazarus raised from the dead, but you have only to show miracles on the screen to obtain something ridiculous. For if miracles are anything, they are mysterious, inscrutable happenings not to be vulgarly approached. The interest of the betrayal and sufferings of Christ was of course different, more real and human, but the bludgeoned audience sat impassively through the dreadful flogging. By slow degrees we approached the Crucifixion. Patricia asked me to take her out and I was glad. It seems to me we should not look on at things we would not ourselves be ready to endure. The Christian sacrifice is in any case not a thing to look on at; it is either something to take part in or it is nothing. We went to 48th Street and drank illicit beer and no cock crew.

I am told that in the final scene Christ is made to rise above the sky-line of New York, the familiar contours of the Woolworth, the Metropolitan, the Paramount, and above them the risen Jesus. So Manhattan was their Golgotha.

CHAPTER XXV

Harlem

BROADWAY is the most sentimental part of New York, the Bowery is the most brutalised, and Harlem is the most vicious. It has an interesting religious and artistic side with which I am not concerned here. The night-life there has a great deal of perversity. This is sex perversion. The Whites who go there rather than the Blacks who live there are to blame for it. Above 125th Street and below 140th Street moral standards are erased. It is New York's red-light district, the equivalent in this great city of the redlight district of the provincial town, until a few years ago a general feature of American urban life. Public opinion on the whole will not tolerate red light districts now. Women lead in cleaning up and men are amenable to their leadership. While the post-war generation of American youth is very vicious, their elders on the side of morality outnumber them by millions. The American ability to look on at vice in Europe and yet not take part in it is always a matter of comment to Europeans and sometimes a cause of cynical jests. The business man lives a strenuous life and expends on his work all that overflowing energy which an idler species is tempted to throw into a bout of sensual pleasure. Not that there are not thousands of exceptions, but the limp male and the Puritan woman predominate.

But New York is out of control. In that respect

and almost in that alone it is not characteristic of America as a whole. The Puritans and the tired business men do not go to Harlem except to see the sights. Its habitués enjoy its perversions. They brag of its colour, its playfulness, its primitiveness, its "high lights." They take foreign visitors there to show them something of America.

There is one big night club which is the *Nigger Heaven, par excellence.* It is unusually sickening. There are those who are sickened by the sight of a naked woman and those who cannot tolerate the public knowledge that men are a mammalian species. America because of her primitive origins has had to be highly perfumed. Hence among other things the draped statues, elaborate bathing-costumes and the infrequency of comfort-stations. But one can be as free in mind as the French and yet be nauseated by Harlem.

The lights are so few that it is almost dark and yet one sees enough. The dancing square is crowded. The music is a harsh staccato punctuated by vociferous horns. All rhythms are blurred. There is no smooth dancing, no gliding, scarcely any forward movement. The dancers hold body to body, they keep on their toes, they sway, they seek contact, they interpret the savage rhythm in sex sensation. Cold partners do not dance there with pleasure. Those who can take pleasure from intimate contact are not content till they have a physical entente and then they let the music do the rest. The dance lasts a long time and coloured lights from a revolving lantern sweep across the faces of the dancers. One of the instruments of the band is a euphonium which with Scriabinesque by-play lights up interiorly in its huge brass mouth with varying coloured lights according to the notes played.

I was there on three nights, first with Nathan Asch, a young novelist, then with Helen when we were greatly disgusted, and thirdly with Jan and Cora Gordon when we stayed till four in the morning witnessing a gala festival of the Monarch Elks. This last proved more interesting because all Harlem seemed to pass in review before us. We saw some marvellous toilets and Jan sketched rapidly all the time, even in the dark. As an experiment I asked an elephantine coloured girl to dance with me. She turned out to be both a housemaid and an Elk. She told me her name was Agnes; she said she had an uncle Stephen. In the first dance she was very aloof, but in the second she determined on a line of action.

"Have yuh any likker, honey?" she enquired.

"Why, no, I'm sorry," said I.

"Will yuh pay fer likker for me?"

I agreed. She danced the rest of the dance with both arms round my neck, much to the ire of a White Southern couple watching us from a table.

At the close of that dance she led me by the hand through the crowded room so that I felt like a small boy being taken out by mother. She went away by the ladies' exit and returned with a quart of gin. It was profusely wrapped in Gordon wrappings and like all Prohibition gin, was contained for convenience in a stoppered bottle . . . no drawing of corks. My coloured partner took a seat at our table and tippled gin from her bottle into our glasses of lemonade. She said that her friends at the next table were "booze poor," so the bottle was also handed to them. They were all good Elks there. Mrs. Gordon drew a picture of Agnes and that enchanted her. She tore out the sheet from the sketch-book and took it to other tables to show it even to strangers. She asked Cora if she might come to her studio and be drawn "real good" some day. Then she folded the drawing in four and put it under her stocking.

The gin-bottle reposed on the floor under the table. A tall policeman was strutting among the bedizened dancers and guests, swinging his nightstick suggestively as if he longed to crack a skull. But his function was the protection of law-breakers; he could only have used his stick upon the virtuous. The club was disobeying the curfew for it was after three o'clock and also there was much open drinking. It was he I think who gave the "up bottles" signal. Waiters with electric torches came searching among the legs of the guests under the tables and made every one pick up his liquor and put it in his pocket. The cop had advised a safety measure.

There were twenty or thirty items of review this night, troops of Negro entertainers arriving from other establishments to honour the Monarch Elks. And even at two and three in the morning there were constant arrivals of new guests, mostly of course black. Some of the women were superbly arrayed; some of the men were wearing dinner jackets. Where we sat, near the entrance and yet facing the middle of the dancing-floor, it was always a great and moving scene. One of the hostesses in black pajamas mingled constantly with the crowd; other hostesses in elegant kimonos sat at tables with guests. In the dim light a marvellous Ethiopian girl with silvered eyelids sang and danced. A naked contortionist tickled her own chin with tenuous fingers of arms which were locked behind her. A stove-black boy with white enamelled lips sang in a voice like three megaphones. A cat-like dwarf girl, the colour of a cocoanut, did the splits on the floor and pulsated with her little stomach and thighs to the heavy music of the winking euphonium. The waiters, wearing low shoes, white gaiters and white smoking caps scooted, dancing, across the floor, bearing above their heads trays with ginger-ale bottles and pots of ice. They stamped, they did step-dances, they surrounded revue-singers, they crouched, they jumped, they flew. Marvellous incredible waiters . . . most of them seemed to have doglike heads which came out of their collars on sinuous doggy necks.

The revues were punctuated with general dancing. An announcer would bawl, "After the next number there will be a stop-down with two encores, after which your kind attention is asked for Marie Antoinette."

Then we were at it again, Whites down on Negro level, Negroes down to Whites' level, darkness, red-flashing lights, insurgent, bombastious, idolatrous trombones and horns, euphonium twinkling like the eye of the obscene, baleful red centre star glowing as if patterned in hell to give the club its due astral influence.

For me the obvious scene faded out and I saw the idol of Nebuchadnezzar, cubits high and the black backs of all the Old Testament idolaters bending before it. I would have liked to see the Three Children walk into the fire and not be burned.

I dare say many people would have given their eyes to see this Monarch Elk gala, but despite the barbaric splendour, the parrot-plumage colours, and the jungle-orgy noise called jazz, I am bound to say that there was much that was vicious and nasty which if described plainly might cause my book to be banned, much that might be phrased *cochonerie minus.*

I felt happier in Harlem outside of night clubs and cabarets. Broad, ill-lit, Lenox Avenue and thousands of Negroes walking on it like shades is one of the most mysterious main streets of America. Africa has become civilised and this is what she has produced. The East Side is Asia merging with Russia. Central New York is Northern and European, septentrional, under the Seven Stars; and Harlem is the South swarming Northward, Africa looking over the Mediterranean, looking over the world. But it is out of place and phantasmal. I always feel that the Old Testament is African much more than Asiatic history. Harlem is like the Old Testament without the Jews. Here are the worshippers of the Calf, no, not the Wall Street calf—we have taken too much to ourselves in identifying Baal-worship with modern business. The chief feature in the adoration of the Calf is a willingness to walk on all fours. At the Harlem River there are few who make a cup of their hands to drink of the water. Solomon goes to Harlem for his Sheba. Samson goes up there when he wants to use the jaw-bone again. The sons of Nimshi drive yellow cabs. The Israelites had a great time killing off the coloured people. They tried to prove they were the Chosen People by exterminating the rest. It was a hopeless task. As well go sweep up the pebbles from the shores of the world. Perhaps the Jews are so pacific to-day because they exhausted the lust for slaughter before the Christian Era. In any case the children of their historic victims survive. "See the hosts of Midian, how they swarm around!"

All the lost tribes prowl up and down Lenox and Seventh Avenue. Men and women with faces like dogs are the most common, descendants of the enslaved, inheriting the bent backs and shapeless enlarged hands of hewers of wood and drawers of water, the rough camaraderie of Babel builders, the beetling brows and big feet of agricultural helots. But there are others who are aristocratic with heathen privilege written on their lips and on their long thin hands. There are robbers and priests, and holders of the mysteries. The genitals of Isis-worship are signed between their eyes. The Sphinx asks his unanswerable question again whenever their faces are at rest.

But of course it is easy to exaggerate. Harlem is not sinister. It is a quaint happy-go-lucky crowd of funnily dressed children with faces like twilight in the evening, like night, like twilight before dawn. They pass and they pass, indolently or hurriedly, as if blown by the wind. There is little of purpose in their lives. They came into being in the United States, they exist, they go on.

In a peep-show on 125th Street I played chess at an open booth. On one side behind a veil was the fat woman; on the other there was a shooting alley. You could play checkers for ten cents and chess for a quarter; you only paid if you lost. Capablanca may have some admixture of Negro blood; most Cubans have. But there are no potential Capablancas in Harlem. My two games proved to be a free entertainment with a "Say, boss, you must be a marster at this game," thrown in in flattery. But playing thus in the open reminded me a little of lands where open-air chess played outside cafés is the chief relaxation of the night.

One of the queerest places in Harlem is called Liberty Hall. White people are not welcomed within its portals. It is the tribunal of the Pan-African movement. The doors stand open at night and peeping in you may see orators in strange robes and hear them guffawing tremendous phrases to a thousand or so advanced Negroes sitting in the seats below. Rows of black women graduates arrayed in their gowns face the audience also and serve to remind that the coloured people can do what white people can do. They cannot quite, of course, but they have their redeeming successes. The orators prate of Liberia and of Haiti as in other parts of the city Russians prate of Moscow and Jews of Zion. Once more you realise the belief in some other country so characteristic of New York. It is sentimental and visionary but it fills a gap and placates the soul.

In thinking of African origins it is easy to overlook the Americanism of the Negro. He is a potent factor in the land. He imitates but he also compels imitation. He has a stronger, simpler face than the white man. His facial contortions and his way of speech are infectious. Modern dance springs from him. I was at the Renaissance Casino and watched men like Mississippi porters, dancing as they would go up the gang-way of a river-steamer balancing cotton-bales and keeping rhythm with their own weird vocal music. And I have seen a pallid reflection of that movement in the dancing in a London club. I have seen the Charleston-lurch without the Charleston and the infection going round the world.

The gliding, prowling, posturing, springing, the

thigh exposures, the hip weaving, the trembling of head and breast in abandonment—how infectious. The white women are much more fastidious than the black, but against their will they want to imitate them. I think that for the original pattern of the "burlesque" dances it is necessary to go to Harlem. The Lafayette Theatre is now given up to Negro Burlesque at fifty cents a seat but the price is no indication of the quality of the dancing you will see. It may be ugly but it is not an imitation of anything. The theatre reeks; you are the only Whites in an ocean of Black, but for fifty cents you obtain a revelation of original burlesque dancing. This in the persons of Florence Mills and her company has been conquering England and France making The Pavilion and the Theatre des Champs Elysées outposts of Harlem in London and Paris.

I danced with a coloured hostess at the Lenox Avenue Savoy. Ruth was a very good dancer but, good mixer as I am, I felt that it was rather a failure. It was like dancing with a big black wooden doll. I think the Northern blond does not easily take to the African. He needs to try it many times before the barriers are broken down. I left Ruth that night but Ruth did not leave me. When I got home I realised I was bathed in a perfume that did not derive from Woolworth. I only danced six dances with her. What must it be like when like the devotees you dance from midnight till breakfast time with coloured partners?

CHAPTER XXVI

The Sugar Cane

EIGHT of us departed one night from Washington Square for Harlem in a taxi. Literary conversation had languished in Louis Weitzenkorn's studio as it is apt to languish at one in the morning, and more highballs and the intrusion of Mrs. Segal's dog did nothing to thwart the desire of the guests to go home. But one of us suggested Harlem and there proved to be magic in the word.

My view as we rushed up the long avenue was the back of the lady who was sitting on me, but an invading glare of lights told of 116th Street, 125th Street as we passed them. We halted on 135th Street to ask the way to the Sugar Cane and then in a minute or so faced the lurid little front of a coloured dive. A name was given to the doorkeeper and we all trooped in. The band was trumpeting like enraged elephants in battle and a gay Negro populace, dressed to the last limit of finery, was swarming in dance. The Sugar Cane premises when empty must look like a wretched club-room for working girls or a place for a Band of Hope to meet. It is a long rectangular area space with low ceiling, worn-out plank flooring, kitchen-chairs and rickety tables. Halfway along in an alcove works the band. The planking of the floor parts, bends and shakes under the dancers.

With laughing obsequiousness a dancing coloured waiter led us to what he thought was the best place in the room, two tables which he cleared of black guests for us. This proved to be exactly opposite the orchestra. Rows of ginger-ale bottles were put in front of us. Louis, who was acting as host to the party, put his private supply of whisky and gin under the table. And each of us led his partner into the mob to dance. To dance under the circumstances was an art apart—no room for turns, no scope for striding, big hips bumping you, awkward shoulders nudging you. You kept your arms down and held your partner close to you, keeping time with sides and knees, dancing statically and ecstatically, imparting and taking rhythm from the breast, from the back, from the thighs, from the middle, ululating forward, ululating back, one's emotions titillated by light strumming, then torn by trumpets. Tall elegant Negresses with carven faces, held by bellicose fighting bulls, sunbonneted mammas with crazy rustic boys, mighty hipped hostesses keeping time by contortioning their buttocks in unison with the males who gripped their waists in the vice of their arms —all these and many others bumped us as we hesitated and wavered in the eddies of the dance.

The Pied Piper led away the children and the rats, the Sugar Cane band brought them back again. Language falls behind that band. What are words like strident, obstreperous, robustious, clamorous to meet this ear-bursting, twangling, miauling invasion of our souls? It tore through the intellect like storm, it entered the belly and burst like wind, it flared like a stick of cordite. It had in it the pugnacious glare of the prize fight, the scream of coloured rape, the yellow frenzy in battle or murder. The piano tattooed on our spines, counting the joints; trumpets spoke to jumping hips, and the curly saxophone, like a harlot's hand, frightened, beguiled and pandered, seeming to say in a suppressed voice, "try fire, try fire."

There were white men dancing with coloured girls, and Negroes dancing with white women, but the most kept to their own colour. Not that we Whites were in any way an adornment of the place; we were really interlopers, we did not belong. The Negroes do not depend on our custom, this is their way of amusing themselves. You change into a bit of a Negro when you join the dance or you do not enjoy it; some of the black comes off on you, none of your white comes off on them.

Some of the Whites were very drunk. One young man lay with his lips to the upper part of the breast of a girl, from two in the morning till about four when he was escorted to a taxi. He was not passionate, he just lay there peacefully and sweetly as if he had found mother, and the girl bore him there impassively at her breast.

Some of the coloured girls seemed very indulgent to their boy friends and their tenderness was curiously out of keeping with their muscular development. Any one of the black girls could have wrestled any two of her white partners.

The waiters brought us round hot barbecue, regular dog's suppers of bones, which we held in our hands picnic-fashion and picked off meat. That washed down with gin and ginger-ale was our chief refreshment. We had perspired in the dance, had forgot the ennui of prolonged literary conversation, had become very thirsty and hungry.

"The joke is when some white man comes down here, gets very drunk and finds himself dancing with his wife's coloured maid," said one of our party. "Or when a white woman discovers that she has 'got off' with the elevator boy from the apartment house where she lives." Many jokes of this sort are possible in mixed company of the kind.

About three a coloured policeman came smirking in, took a drink, looked us over and then slunk out. The curfew order had lately been imposed and all places of amusement were supposed to close their doors at three o'clock. The policeman's visit symbolised the curfew. We did not close our doors. It was sometime after four with the music still blaring that we filed out, bundled into a taxi and crossed the Congo, 125th Street, leaving the black compound behind to enter once more the domain of civilisation.

CHAPTER XXVII

Exclusive!

"YOU'RE not a dawg catcher, are ye?"

These words were addressed to me by a loafer outside the brightly illuminated entrance of a cross-street club in Harlem. The Negro porter found difficulty in admitting me and had gone to talk to the boss. But the loafer, a white man, also was in the club's employ and mistook me for a revenue officer. When I explained that I was English he said:

"Well, I guess that's all right. Come off a ship, eh? Well, all you have to do is to grease the nigger's hands. Right Joe, he's O. K."

I found the grease and was then affably welcomed by the door-keeper who took me downstairs.

A clerk handed me a statement to read over which looked like the Declaration of Independence. "This heah's an exclusive club," said he. "Yuh cahn get in unless yuh sign the rules." I was asked to fill in a form which among other things said: "If you are naturalised state when you took out your papers and where."

"I can't fill this up. I'm a foreigner," said I with relief.

"All right, boss," said the clerk affably. "Just sign over that number and pay a dollar."

So after all I was admitted.

The Club was in a gaily-adorned, beautifully painted cellar. There were tables all around, there was a pit with a jazz band in it, and in the centre pranced coloured girls, some in pink satin pyjama trousers, others in roseate knickers. The company was white; the entertainment was black. Negro waiters danced about with tiny straw hats on the sides of their fuzzy heads. I sat down and ordered a bottle of beer, but I felt somewhat abashed and not quite at home when a voluptuous pagan at once shimmied to my knees and languished up toward my face.

To cover embarrassment I wanted to say, "Take a seat, girlie," but the words froze on my lips.

My neighbour at the next table appeared to be a "butter and egg" man. He had come from Indianapolis for a three days' business spree in New York, and I gathered from his remarks that the capital of Indiana did not offer him as much scope for his way of enjoying himself. His style was not that of New York. There was something agricultural about him, as if some of the earth of the corn country still adhered to his boots. His square-cut clothes were Pullman ironed. He had thick hands and stubby wooden-looking fingers. The sight of him there with his wad of dollars in front of him reminded me that the night resorts are not exclusively patronised by New Yorkers and the explanation of their type of entertainment is not to be found entirely in the need of New York to escape from New York. Despite the reiterated statement that you must not judge America by New York there are many Americans ready to come to New York in order to forget America.

They bury the Middle West in New York. For, despite the wildness of night-life in Chicago you cannot quite bury the Middle West anywhere there. They try to bury it in Chicago and then re-bury it in New York. New York is big enough to lose Babbitt in.

But Babbitt bobs up in the night club, and here he was in Harlem. To an outsider his behaviour was part of the show and it would have been worth an extra dollar for his part in it.

There were fifteen coloured girls, all of them young and good-looking. The man from Indianapolis had his bootleg flask whose contents he tilted out in cascades into his glass. The girls in turn danced up to him so close that they were nose to nose and knee to knee, and each, fingering her one garment unlaced it in front of him, and when she had done so to his satisfaction he lifted a bill from the table and solemnly presented it to her.

The girls snatched the bills in a graceless way, much as fawning dogs almost bite the fingers which give them bread. Their massive eyebrows hid the avid look in their eyes, but their lithe bodies as they at once retreated expressed contempt for the giver and scarcely contentment with the gift. They were not sensual, not lustful—their posturing was mechanical, a technical manipulation of a man to get his dollars from him. Again and again they went up to him, did their trick, postured and got their bills.

One of them with a five-dollar bill in her hand,

THE SUGAR CANE
Ethiopia entertains Solomon at 135th Street.

the Sheba of this Solomon, came Charlestoning from him to me, so closely I could feel her breathing, and looked at me so intently as her legs trembled and her body shook that I felt she was not using her eyes but was looking at me with her shapely thick-lipped compelling mouth. Her face at close quarters was like that of a shaved cat, very African and jungly. She possessed a hypnotic glare, and I involuntarily whispered as she moved away from me three lines of Lindsay's, *"Mumbo-Jumbo who lives in the jungle, Mumbo-Jumbo will hoo-do-o you."* But the trick did not work on me. As the Scotch saying goes, "Ye canna tak' the breeks aff a Hielander." I felt the pull all the same, I want a dollar, I want a dollar. What shall I do to lift a dollar from you? But I hadn't any dollars to dispense, valuable as her performance was in the forming of my impressions of New York at night.

The parade of girls gave way to a mêlée of dance. Coloured paper hats were brought in to disguise us, make us not what we were, destroy the validity of our passports, dissociate us from the implications of our drab clothes. Babbitt with a flaming red topper still remains Babbitt, you will say. But I think that, adding something to him, you take something away. Babbitt minus is more amusing than Babbitt plus. I am so much of a Puritan I do not like to put on a bibulous cardboard nose, and so much of a Catholic that I won't wear a hat while I eat. But when I took off the monstrous hat which my waiter had affectionately and facetiously placed on my brows, he hurried back, replaced it, and waggishly slapped my head. Some other guests who took off their hats got slapped too. That slap seemed to fix the hats on for good. After that they stayed on; we dared not remove them.

The coloured lights were turned out and instead four spot-lights played on the centre of the room out of the dark corners. We were given coloured balloons, squeakers, and rolls of coloured strips of paper. Every one began squeaking, and burst balloons were popping. The voices and laughter of the crowd imitated the squeaks and the pops. It grew very noisy with variegated noises, very lurid with variegated gaudiness, guests and girls threw their bodies and limbs about, jumping, arm-waving, shaking. Glasses clinked and bottles dipped, and black heads like rich shadows flirted with pale moonlike faces. The waiters with their little straw hats grew gayer and gayer and put whisky flasks in our side pockets with the gestures of ballet or pantomime.

Out came a wild array of good-looking children of joy, dancing as they sang, shouting, posturing, contorting, and going through those African rituals so well described in Batouala. What they did is almost indescribable. They reproduced dance rhythms with every curve of their bodies. The Black Bottom may imitate the movements of ooze in the river bed. Their ventral movements reminded one of the movement of canoes in turbulent waters. Front seemed to float or back slip away off fast moving waves. Tip-tilted chins, circling bosoms, agitated knees, slipping heels, and roof-raising clamour of saxophones and human laughter and song! The white guests threw serpentines of coloured paper across and across till every girl was incredibly tangled; we blew out our balloons, squeaked on the squeakers, burst balloons with re-sounding pops, shouted and sang and drank. The flasks were handed to the half-demented band and to the chorus girls, and the scene ceased to be one of dance. The romp ran itself. It was a runaway. The horses were running away with the sledges.

This, in its variations, went on an hour or so, and the waiters dancing in with the girls got as lively as the girls, and carried the Club president, a ponderous African, round the room, holding him by his knees so that his huge body swayed about as if it were a stuffed figure. Then the Whites got up and danced with the coloured girls, then there was the Black Bottom and a rivalry in solo dances and repellent contortionism, and every time a girl "rang the bell" with some unusually daring show-off the solemn gentleman from Indiana with the decaying wad of dollars got to, solemnly interrupted the dance, and presented the girl with a bill.

Most of the girls took their tips across to the piano-player in the band, and he stowed them away in his capacious pockets.

The waiter came up to me.

"Hope yo's 'joyin' yosef, boss," said he. "Any gal you like you c'n have, jus' lemme know."

Presently I had a rather cute, breathless, perspiring hussy sitting at my table drinking "inspiration," where I was drinking inspiration of a different kind.

Something curious was yet to happen. Two small boys came in, and the girls left the centre of the club and sat on white men's knees or leaned against them with their arms round their necks, lipping cigarettes and blowing the white smoke into their partner's eyes. The painted cellar at that time was full of tobacco smoke and whisky fumes and odours of other kinds. It was nearing three o'clock, and into this strange atmosphere and Bacchic scene came two children and sang "blues" to us in piping treble.

They were made up like girls. Anti-kink had been applied to their hair. They faced one another and "performed" in a grown-up professional way. I saw their jazz mothers in their lineaments, their jazzing fathers too. From the womb to the cabaret—what a short way! They had an exaggerated success. The drunkard was made tender and emotional, the man from Indianapolis handed a waiter money to give them; every one found something for the boy singers and, self-satisfied and smiling, they strutted out of the room. Neither was more than twelve years old, and I wondered what they did with the money so easily earned and what their future would be.

I talked afterwards to the police at Headquarters about these singers, and one told me how he had arrested a Negro boy of the kind about four o'clock one morning in Harlem. He found that the boy went from club to club all night, taking a taxi each time. He was so little he was provided with a stick with which to reach up to the bells on the club doors. He had over a hundred dollars in his possession; he appeared to be a child without father or mother, and lived more or less on his own. Not a child that father and mother would desert, you would think, but he started his profession singing for nickels outside theatres and graduated to the cabaret and the club. The police set the little waif singer at liberty but something of his story was reported in the press.

The children however were quickly forgotten in this club. The waiters sang instead. Indeed, the waiters had a very good time, combining with their table service the functions of entertainers and the pleasures of the guests. They danced, they sang, they got drunk, but they also collected their tips. The floor was covered with confetti, burst balloons, and paper hats, but they did not bring brooms and sweep it clear. And when the band rested the waiters improvised on their trumpets and saxophones.

There seemed to be no control, but there was no fight. The good-natured president went to various tables and drank with his guests, petted and patted and purring, his great frame in voluminous black frock-coat, looking like a human wall. The girl with the face like a shaved cat seemed to be his favourite, sang to him repeatedly and heaved her great bosom in front of him, as if over-confident of her beauty and desirability.

I caught the coat tail of a dancing waiter, gave him ten dollars, and went home. A few steps and the highly coloured scene with its lights and its noise was shut off. One emerged into the grey darkness of the ordinary world at three in the morning. The tropics were changed for New York. Instead of roseate Bougainvillæas—the gloomy wood and iron Elevated Railway, Lenox Avenue, Seventh Avenue, rain-washed and depopulated, trailed on in the dark. The subway was dreary beyond words. I changed and waited at 91st Street. Still away at the club they kicked the confetti around, the lights converged on the bacchantes, the great black president murmured in converse with his guests. But the seats on the subway station were occupied by homeless men stretched out full length and sleeping. For lack of something to do I weighed myself and found I had lost eight pounds during the evening. It was tedious, unsatisfactory, empty. The Negro night club made one less at home with New York. Its drabness had become intensified. There is no refuge for the soul in a subway station. Why should there be? It is a bare utility. I put a penny in another automat and received a sugar-coated piece of gum. I found another weighing machine and found I had lost four more pounds. The train came at last, and the passengers sprawled and slept —and the conductor between stations took a seat in the train opposite me and slept too. I bought a morning paper and read the latest details of the latest murder. Newsvendors with the Tabloid press wandered up and down the train crying the "Graphic" and the "News." I sat and stared at "Going-going-gone"—the advertisement of the man with herpes of the scalp. It mocked the bald man on my left, but he slept. All the passengers slept—on their way to work, most of them, and beginning the mechanical routine of the day with somnambulism. I got out at 33rd Street and walked through dead and sleeping Gimbel's. There is a sky-sign above the slope of Murray Hill—the number 72 in electric lamps in the sky. That came to be my sky-sign, for I lived so near it. It surmounts the barracks of the 72nd Regiment, the Armoury, and assists boys if they lose themselves before reveille, a sign set in the heavens to show them the way home.

So I reached that bulwark of the Avenue and also my own home, and worked the elevator myself and hoisted myself up to the top floor, and was very quickly abed, dreaming quaintly of shaved cats and coloured girls dancing around the fat black president of an exclusive Harlem club. Dreamland is nearer Nigger Heaven than New York.

CHAPTER XXVIII

Second Half of the Night

I RECEIVED an introduction to a place called The Second Half of the Night; it was merely a sentence scribbled in pencil on the back of the card of a Negro undertaker:—"Friend Jack, this is one of my friends."

This was a resort kept by an Italian whose wife was French. The wife was chief hostess and a fine singer—at least, so I was informed. The entrance was from a dingy street in Greenwich Village. Helen was my partner, a young artist on "The World," and together we sought out "Friend Jack."

Jack seemed by no means pleased to see us, and we were disappointed by the look of his place. It appeared to be a restaurant; it was white-walled, untidy, chill and empty.

"Do you not have music and dancing?" I asked.

He looked at me in a pained way as if several of his teeth were aching at once.

"Used to have," said he. "But it's been closed up some months now."

I looked surprised.

"Oh, well, it does not matter," said I, preparing to go out again. "But the other night in Harlem I met a friend of yours and he recommended the place strongly. As a matter of fact he gave me a note to you."

I fumbled among the many cards I had already collected in New York. Jack looked on gloomily.

"Ah, here it is," said I. " 'Friend Jack, this is one of my friends.' "

I handed it to him.

"Who give you that?" he asked.

I told him.

"All right," said he. "Follow me."

He then led us by a side door into a dark hallway and down the length of it till he came to a small padlocked gate, and by that he conducted us into a barn-like room illuminated by Chinese lanterns and wall lights. The walls had been luridly painted by some Village artist and shewed horned gentlemen and nymphs among trees. The ceiling was covered with autumn leaves.

There were but two couples besides ourselves in the room and they were sitting in a far corner sipping red wine. The ladies were fat and dark; their companions were swarthy men, evidently Italians. A cushioned bench ran round the room. Tiny tables were placed close to this bench and there was a narrow space left for dancing in the centre of the floor.

Friend Jack asked us what we would take, but at that point in the adventure he was still suspicious of us and would not give us cocktails. He brought us ginger-ale instead. This implied no loss to him for he charged us the same price.

Five small Italian men and one very large woman then entered and they ordered a full-course dinner with cocktails and red wine. Following them came two couples; evidently they had already been drinking as they were very noisy, and they brought their own whisky with them. The girls were exceedingly abandoned. They took a table opposite us and we watched their embraces and listened to the back chat. Other guests, mostly Latin in appearance, came in and the place began to be quite lively.

The music was furnished by a pale and impressive young man who played a small grand piano in a mechanical way, seated under a spotlight.

Jack's wife, huge, diamonded, painted, began to sing. Was it singing? It was rather vocal percussion. It was active singing. Her songs struck you. They caused breezes. Her bosom, ill-confined in her low-cut evening frock, rose and fell as her music was discharged at us.

"Chérie, je t'aime [*Sherree dje tame*]"—it hit us between the eyes.

But at the same time she smiled ingratiatingly. She did not mean to assault her guests. She was a good mixer and very clever in keeping every one in a good humour and in lifting dollars for Friend Jack.

We began to realise that the club was now divided into two camps; one of the rather silent Italians, the other of the two gay couples facing us and ourselves. I said to Helen, "We are in with a rough crowd and we don't belong here at all. I should not be surprised if there were trouble later on. We had better keep very much to ourselves. Let us act like two people who are not interested in any one else in the world but one another."

So Helen and I sat close and exchanged confidences like lovers and were enough unto ourselves, watchfully taking in the changing scene nevertheless.

But we were destined to be made one with the rest of the people in the room, and it was largely due to one of the gay girls opposite us. She was dancing between drinks and waving a coat-hanger, singing snatches of Russian and American airs, picking up her skirt with one hand and kneeing it round the room. Presently she espied my old tweed hat which was lying on the cushioned bench beside us, ran over, put it jauntily on the side of her bobbed head, and did an apache turn in it. Her partner reproached her with interfering with other people's property, but she paid no attention. He looked at me. I said it did not matter. And then he left his table; came over and sat beside me.

He was a slim young man of twenty-six or seven, neatly dressed. His face was grey, lined, educated. His eyes were pocketed, his lips weak and wet. He did not really look at me. It was with averted eyes he began the conversation.

"What do you think of her, of Rose-Marie?" he asked.

I was surprised by the question. If one takes out a girl one hardly asks a stranger his opinion of one's partner. So I answered him cautiously.

"She seems very gay and amusing," said I.

He was silent a moment or so, watching the antics of Rose-Marie, who had noticed at once he was talking about her and made her comment by posturing audaciously in front of us.

As she moved off he turned to me and whispered impressively:

"She's a curse."

"How's that?" I enquired. "She looks very charming."

"She's a curse. But for her I would be with my wife in Oregon. Every day I say, 'To-morrow I'll be at the Grand Central with my things, pulling out for the North-West and home.' But every night finds me out on another jaunt with Rose-Marie."

"I am a month overdue," he went on. "I have a wife and child and there's another one just coming. What do you think of it? And I am a doctor. Where's my ambition, my profession? How can I get away? What would you advise me to do?"

It is of no use advising a man in that state to go back to his wife and child. So I said, "A month with Rose-Marie would be worth years with your wife, I've no doubt."

"Oh, no," said he, "I love my wife passionately."

Then he told me that the two girls were Russians, and that they were sisters, and that the other man was a doctor also and both from the same town.

"Was Rose-Marie born in Russia?"

"No, in the Bronx, where she lives now."

At that point Rose-Marie came up to the table and restored my hat to me with a flourish, took a seat in front of me and bent her passionate orbs upon me.

"You look sort of cute," said she. "Ask me a question?"

Thus challenged to say something smart I smiled at her and enquired:

"Did you ever bathe in the Harlem River?"

At this surprise question she started, put her chubby face in her hands, and had a long convulsion of flapper's mirth. Then she raised her face, smoothing imaginary tears from her cheeks, and replied:

"Let me tell you, Mr. Man, I have bathed in every bit of water in this country except the Pacific Ocean, and I mean to bathe there before long."

"Oh, the North Pacific, the coast of Oregon," said I laughingly.

Therese at this point began to bellow forth in song, drowning conversation. Rose-Marie beckoned to her sister and the other doctor and they joined us at our table. Rose-Marie's partner sat next to Helen on the other side and began to court her. He was evidently an incurable.

"Now you ask me a question," said I to Rose-Marie.

"What are you doing here?" she asked.

"Snooping around," I replied.

Rose-Marie was pretty but her sister was beautiful; she had a calm, smooth, oval face and long, tapering, artistic hands.

"Do you know what we said about you?" enquired Rose-Marie. "We said, 'Look at them; they are the only sensible people in the room. They have come in for a long talk and not to make fools of themselves.'"

Helen smiled. We had really succeeded in our pose of being wrapped up in one another.

The other doctor emptied the last drips of his whisky into our ginger-ale. He was a burly, good-natured fellow, but he did not give himself away as did Rose-Marie's partner.

The sister too had composed her much-kissed lips and was now behaving very steadily.

Helen, who is a student of hands, pointed to those of the sister with admiration.

"Yes," I said, "she might show her hands to Duse."

"Oh!" exclaimed the sister. "Say something more about my hands, if you understand them."

"You are amusing. We compare your hands with those of Eleonora Duse and you are not satisfied. You want something more."

I took one of her hands in mine, opened it, and began to tell her her character. Helen took the doctor's and did the same.

At this the whole room seemed to sense what we were doing and every one in the place crowded round us and thrust out their hands to be read; the swarthy Italians, the fat women, the waiters, the piano player, Jack's wife, Jack himself.

What Helen was saying I do not know, but I was kept busy giving enigmatic or striking characterisations. The men had very hard fists full of driving power, violence and unruly temper, contrasting curiously with the babyish and flabby hands of their women partners.

A short peppery Italian brought his huge dark mistress to me. "Tell her something," he ordered.

Her palms looked as if they had not yet dried out after a long immersion in warm water. I looked at them for some time and then daringly remarked:

"You are not a passionate woman."

This provoked mirth.

"That's all you know about her," said the little Italian.

"If you seem to have passion it comes out of bottles. It does not come out of yourself," I corrected.

"Out of bottles," said Jack's wife. "That's good."

"You are not a volcano. Your passion is on draught."

Her man, made curious by this, thrust his hand out.

"Well," said I, "you are a gambler in life. But you always gamble on something which will bring you nothing worth having if you win."

And so on. We had quite a success. Friend

Jack had no more suspicions about us. We got a bottle of wine. The doctors got more whisky. Rose-Marie's partner took out Helen to dance. I talked to Rose-Marie. She gave her version of the story of herself and her doctor-lover.

"I'm a nurse," she said, and tittered. "And I am *very* professional. Don't think I'm like this on the hospital floor. I am always correct. Harry saw me one day in one of the wards and he'd no sooner set eyes on me than he came right up to me and said, 'Gee, I think you're the most beautiful girl I ever saw in my life.' I was so scared I didn't know what to say. He followed me out of the hospital and I ran. He came running after me but I wouldn't speak to him. Next day it was the same. He wouldn't let me alone. So I let him take me out if Vera came too. Then he brought Sherman and Sherman fell in love with Vera at first sight, and here we are."

Rose-Marie gave a long nervous giggle. Her admirer had brought Helen back and we said no more about the story. Helen seemed somewhat dismayed by the dance. Really it was she who had brought the doctor back, having found that he was too unsteady for movement and too amatory for pleasure. Seated beside her the doctor wished to encircle Helen's waist with his arm, but she held him off, amusingly saying, "If you feel that way you can hold my hand, but no more."

There was a loud knocking at the door at this point, and some one said, "Valentino is knocking," at which the singing wife of the proprietor called out to the company, "No, we've got no dead ones here."

The mother of a fashionable actor came in. She was grey-haired, well-dressed, and very drunk. Her escort was a short rock-like man who was lame. They made a very grotesque couple. A woman from Kansas City came in and talked to us. She hoped the club might be raided, and asked us to realise that she was risking a home and husband for this one night. She was fat and middle-aged but well corseted. She danced with all the Italians and was purposefully gay, twiddling her gartered knee, and shewing the undulatory elegancies of her person. Many new people seemed to have come in unnoticed by us and there was now a severe-looking old lady at one of the tables who said nothing but nursed her repressed lips and eyed Helen with a pitying air.

A Salvation Army officer came in and began selling papers, but he addressed no one on the state of his soul.

The doctor seemed to have forgotten Rose-Marie, for he was making most unwelcome advances to Helen. I looked him over with equanimity—if necessary I felt I should have no difficulty in knocking him down. Helen and I were not on terms of closest intimacy, but I realised that if you take a lady to a night club you must be prepared to protect her from insult.

So I put a proprietary arm round my little artist. At that the doctor became extremely morose and pushed the roses which were on the table far away from him.

"They remind me of funerals," said he.

He then turned out all his pockets, looking for money which was not there, and he asked querulously who would pay for the drinks. The other doctor had also spent most of his money.

A girl in a blue velvet dress came over to admire my moustache and drink some of our hooch. She asked if she might call her "boy-friend" to our table. He was dressed in a loud black-and-white check and looked like a bookmaker.

"So you all come from out West?" said he. "Well, folk, I've a terrible black cross against my name."

"How's that?"

"I come from Brooklyn," he explained apologetically.

The second half of the night was far gone. I asked the doctors if they had enough to pay their large bill, and we found that Jack was willing to accept a cheque. So that solved that problem. I paid mine, and with many parting greetings led Helen away from the sentimental lover of Rose-Marie, out into the dingy sleeping street where cats were prowling among the garbage cans, and home. We promised Rose-Marie and the sister and the doctors to meet many times. But of course we never did. I suppose we shall never see them again. I hope two wives in Oregon will have been indulgent to errant husbands staying too long, caring for the health of New York!

CHAPTER XXIX

A New-Yorker Free-for-All

THE Vienna Hall, derelict, almost half-seas-over. In the basement a barrel of beer on trestles, hot dogs galore, sandwiches and rows of Scotch. All who have ever contributed to the smartest of New York weeklies have been invited to a free-for-all, and they have come with their friends. Up above the hot-dog parlour is a spacious reception room in the midst of which is a band whose high-ball glasses look like so many unlit fairy lamps. The first fiddle stamps the time, dances and waves his wand. Half the world is dancing.

Literary Bohemia is amusing itself. The women are dressed and the men are handsomely untidy. Unlike London whose literary world is recluse, suburban and dull, but more like Paris, New York can muster at will anywhere and on any occasion a lively many-coloured crowd. But as everywhere the literary crowd looks rather mouldy, as if drawn from gloomy attics. A man who has lost a suspender comes with one sock loose, one tight. Fountain-pens are visible. When coats flap manuscripts are seen in inside-pockets. I see men with proof-reading eyes. I see many whose currency is wit, to whom an epigram is more than a meal, dealers in words and witticisms, satire and slang. Patricia and I, not being sure whether it is a greater mark of respect to come as we are, have taken a chance and are both untidy.

She wears her Shanghai Gesture, a necklet of pearls given her once by one of the contributors upon his return from Shanghai. While the said contributor is renewing acquaintance and flirting with her, some one picks his pockets imitating the youngest Marx brother in the Cocoanuts. He has hardly recovered his handkerchief of blue, when he finds he has lost his pocket-toothpick, and as he gets that back he loses a manuscript. Yes, he was dancing with a short story in his pocket. That is to be literary. "Those who have not dressed for the party belong to the élite," says a stout illustrator in grey serge very encouragingly. But the editor was dressed and there was a fixed smile on his face all night like an illuminated "Welcome" sign.

On the arm of a man-eating brunette sails one of the pale collaborators of *Whoops, Dearie!* Mrs. Angell is eating angel-cake. The leading lady of the *Green Hat,* herself in green, smiles and smiles as I pass on the dance-floor. "Yes, I am stuck on the title of my novel, *Intimate Acrobatics,"* says a young writer. Will not his next be *Loving Wrestlers?* The orchestra is playing the popular airs from *Hit the Deck,* and twenty or thirty couples are hitting it.

Snatches of conversation overheard seem strangely irrelevant. "Yes, I am writing the biography of a clergyman who fell in love forty times. A clergyman has an emotional experience every week. You cannot go on preaching sermons out of yourself. You must have a woman's emotions to draw upon" . . . "Please don't call me Mr. Bones. My name is really Jones" . . . "I had to use mad money on Tuesday night. Lucky I always carry five dollars mad money in case of need" . . . "I am disgusted with men since I read Sinclair Lewis's book. Every man I see looks like Elmer Gantry."

In the centre of a group stands Gene Tunney in evening dress so unlike every one else that it seems he ought to have a ticket on him marked *Imported.* Against the physical background of Bohemia he looks superhuman, godlike. He is tall and square, florid yet fresh. All the contributors together could not push him over. But Tunney is happy as a child to be among literary folk. Like Frederick the Great he would like to write a sonnet. No doubt many males looking at him have the opposite ambition and would gladly throw away cap and bells and fountain pen to "pack his wallop." I gave him a shove but he did not budge. He said he had read one of my books on tramping; he would go tramping with me. This with boyish enthusiasm; he had been week-ending with Vachel Lindsay in the Far West and had discussed a tramping triumvirate . . . just too flattering to the capacities of the poet and myself. "Meet Pat," said I. "All the ladies are your admirers. It must be a terrible nuisance to you. But there you are."

"On the contrary," said Gene, blushing.

"Oh, cut that newspaper stuff. We know all about it."

Smiling, we parted.

CHAPTER XXX

Bleecker

AT midnight under a lamp post on Bleecker Street Edgar Allan Poe wrote those famous lines, "Once upon a midnight dreary, while I pondered weak and weary upon many a quaint and curious volume of forgotten lore," and went on to compose the first draft of "The Raven." Now on the corner of Bleecker and Mulberry there is a dark window full of stuffed owls and white rats.

I was down there at midnight seeking the spot where this piece of divine melancholy came to birth. Was it where now stands Perazzo's Funeral Church with its ashy-yellow alabaster urns illuminated from within? Or was it at the eastern end where the drunkards stagger home from the unclosed Bowery bars? Or was it where a fading star on a tented doorway shows the way to Mori's?

Children have lighted fires collecting the street garbage together; the night-wind fans the flames. Continuous reverberating hootings echo off the level sheets of water as unseen ferry-boats arrive or take off. Poe's friends whom he had deserted drove home up Broadway on a bumping horse-bus. Now street-cars come skating along the centre of the empty roadway. Bleecker at midnight is dreary enough and mysterious enough now to inspire the writer of "The Raven," what with its black, dead, shadowy warehouses and the howls of the ferry-boats. At the corner of Wooster you look down to the illuminated rigging, cabins and sails of a tall ship. No, not a ship, an office building with the lights left in many rooms and on many floors after the toilers have gone home.

One half of the street is plunged in gloom, the other half is still alive with vendors of spaghetti and spumoni. There are so many policemen swinging their night-sticks that one expects some midnight brawl. In the background there are stores of forbidden wine. Behind closed shutters and drawn blinds one hears noisy Italians. Overhead trains crash into the old brown elevated station.

But in the quiet gloomy half of the street there are still standing some of the houses of Poe's day, crazy old houses inhabited by day, uninhabited by night, and there the raven still is sitting, never flitting, and the only word there spoken is the whispered name Lenore. I always thought that Poe must have written his poem in his own study late, in an ecstasy of self-banishment. But now I see that it did not come exclusively out of his own heart. New York wrote it, Bleecker Street wrote it. There are roots of poetry under the paving of the "Village."

CHAPTER XXXI

Lighted Rafts

IF New York were an ancient city it would undoubtedly be walled and gated and at the gateways there would be ladders and landing-stages which could be lowered or withheld at will. The bridges and ferry-stations of New York as it is are symbols of portals which might have been. Because of its high buildings it is a city of walls; it exposes more of sheer wall than any other city in the history of the world. It seems to have its defences. It is built against the wind and the slings and arrows of Fate. A panoramic view heroically designed should show a very noble city. I see the little island crowded with great houses even to the water's edge, conventional curling waves and on these waves at the right intervals, ferry-boats going to the other shore or returning from the main-land. Liners going and coming might also be shown looking like larger ferry-boats; for they are Atlantic ferries taking people back and forth between Europe and America every day of the week.

The ferries are a very important pictorial part of New York. Without them she would be like a fly without legs. Without them the city would be moribund as if nothing came out of her and nothing came in. They indicate life and movement. All day and all night they cross and recross and we know the city has life, is receiving life, is giving life. I think that perhaps there is more poetry in the aspect of the ferry-boats at night than in anything else in New York.

125TH STREET FERRY
Where the Palisades sends its searchlights to the stars.

One of the most mysterious is the Fort Lee ferry at 125th Street. You sail up Riverside Drive on the top of an omnibus and the Hudson glitters all the way to Grant's Tomb. On your left in the sky but over the water gleams a palace or a city of lights . . . ten thousand lights resplendently massed, and towards this peak of illumination glide fairy-boats. As you get nearer the boats are seen to be much more substantial and the lighted palace is seen to be composed of two towers, an electric fountain and a great wheel. There are blue-lighted factory windows below. You take the ferry and you are on the way to the Palisades Amusement Park.

There is a feeling of embarkation as if one were actually passing along the gang-way of a ship that was going to take one away from New York. The feet on the dank drab decks sense the water underneath. You think involuntarily of a cabin. You look over the side of the boat much as a dog looks out from a motor when he has been lifted on to a seat and he thinks with pleasure that presently he will feel himself moving. There is a feeling of adventure and movement. The eyes rest pensively on the silver and sepia wash. Ah, but it is only a trip to the Palisades. Yonder is the gaudy lurid show which you are moving almost insensibly but nevertheless steadily towards. The halo in the sky above it is like a roof of light.

A ferry from the other side approaches and passes like a subway train on the waters, long progressive lines of lighted windows on the flattened river and silver lines below slipping away.

And we are at the other side and wind out into a waiting trolley car which groans upward on the loops of the steeply graded track to the cliff where all the razzle-dazzles are. That is not so interesting. The Great Wheel is seen to be slowly revolving; the towers are those of a Scenic Railway; sailors and their girls are shooting the rapids, for the Fleet is in New York harbour and all the jolly tars have shore-leave. Each has found a girl and is playing "Dodge 'em" with her, or "Skee-ball," or "Whip." They are bumping into one another in the tri-cars on the electric floors; they are trying to win prizes at the hazards and the lotteries. They are dancing in the open-air dance hall. They are screaming and singing and flirting and giggling. I feel that I have drawn a blank in this wonderland, turn my back on it and face New York again.

What a walk it is down to the shore! All the great city in banks and shoals of lights. I thought of the millions of human beings there. Every spark was as it were an illuminated human heart. And that darkness of background against which it shone was like the stretch of oblivion upon which we write in brilliant fading characters our little lives and histories.

THE END

www.ingramcontent.com/pod-product-compliance
Lightning Source LLC
LaVergne TN
LVHW010546110826
845149LV00003B/582